SECURED POSSESSION

Gillian Baxter

Copyright © 2023 Gillian Baxter

All rights reserved

The characters and events portrayed in this book are fictitious. Any similarity to real persons, living or dead, is coincidental and not intended by the author.

No part of this book may be reproduced, or stored in a retrieval system, or transmitted in any form or by any means, electronic, mechanical, photocopying, recording, or otherwise, without express written permission of the publisher. The only exception is by a reviewer, who may quote short excerpts in a review.

CONTENTS

Title Page
Copyright
Chapter one   1
Chapter two   18
Chapter three   33
Chapter four   52
Chapter five   69
Chapter six   80
Chapter seven   100
Chapter eight   127
Chapter nine   145
Chapter ten   152
Chapter eleven   168
Chapter twelve   181

CHAPTER ONE

Nell was missing again. Her foal, the little white mule Muff, was in the field, un-worried by the disappearance of her mother. She had the two donkeys for company and Buzz was more of a guardian to her than the mare. Muff was more or less weaned, having learned to fend for herself on these occasions when her mother went walkabout. The one-eyed grey pony had always disliked being fenced in since the time she had spent on a tether and half starved. Patsy sighed and resigned herself to a walk down to the wood before breakfast.
'Not again,' her husband, Mack, came out of the barn stable where he had been feeding the three horses who were in at night, his own Osbourne and Patsy's cob Goliath and her ex-racehorse Lad.
'I think she goes looking for Forrest,' Patsy told him. 'He first put her there, she foaled down there, and now she's seen him down there again she goes searching.'
'I can't imagine my old boy bothering to go looking for me,' Mack joined her by the gate. 'But then he's never been in a state to need rescuing, unlike your unicorn.'
Patsy was not so sure, Mack and his old horse were very close, but she laughed, remembering her first

sight of the grey mare in the windy moonlight.

'Some unicorn,' she said. 'A one-eyed renegade. I'd better go and haul her back. Huw wouldn't be happy to find her on that bit of land.'

'No, he'd have the conservation people after him for endangering those rare lichens.' Mack gave her a hug. 'Go on then, 'I'll get some breakfast going, bacon do?'

Patsy assured him that it would.

He turned towards the house, still an attractive man in his sixties with his wavy greying hair and upright carriage, and Patsy watched him affectionately for a moment before picking up a head collar and starting down the stoney path down to the wooded ravine and the stream. Marriage to Mack might have come late in her life but it was no less close or passionate because of that and he was a dab hand with the frying pan.

It was almost the end of winter now, the stormy weather of West Wales at least briefly settled, the sun bright and the trees showing the first sign of green. The clouds of white blossom on the blackthorn had transformed the winter dark slopes of the ravine and the stream was running fast and full, Patsy could hear it as she reached the green strip between trees and water. The pony was there, a grey mixture of Welsh breeds, tearing at the wet grass, and as she heard Patsy coming she threw up her head, turning it so that her good eye was towards the approaching footsteps.

'Yes, it's me,' Patsy told her. 'Not your dear Forrest I'm afraid. Maybe he'll come to see you later.'

For a moment she thought that Nell, named after Nelson for her one eye, was going to walk away but then she held out a carrot and the pony thought better of it. Patsy slipped the head collar on and together they started back up the steep path to where Mack would have bacon waiting.

It was a comfortable breakfast, eaten in the cosy back room of the cottage with its warmly humming old Rayburn and its faithful family of cats. Afterwards Patsy did a quick washing up while Mack, who wrote popular thrillers, went up to the little room in which he had his word processor and a supply of coffee making equipment, and then she stepped into her boots and went to turn out the three stabled horses. She also had to collect her grandson from the cottage in the converted old stable where her daughter and her husband lived with their small son. It was his other grandmother, Rhianne's, turn to baby sit him this morning while a Katy sat at her computer dealing with her online I.T. adviser work.

Buzz was at his gate as Patsy crossed the yard, his long ears pricked as he saw her. Muff was lying down near old Jack the other donkey, who had got her mother in foal before his previous

owner had 'had him dealt with' as he put it. The little dog with whom he had liked to play had returned to London with her owner as the COVID risk became less and his old donkey companion Harley had died and now Buzz sometimes seemed to be at a loose end. For many years he and Harley had travelled shows and parties with their old owner, giving rides to children, and he had been used to change and attention. Pausing to stroke him Patsy had an idea.

Buzz's old saddle and bridle were in the tack room and it was quite a long walk to Rhianne's, usually it meant taking Tomos's buggy and waiting for him to toddle alongside until he got tired. He had sat on Buzz in the field, why shouldn't he sit there for longer?

'Come on, let's see how you do as transport,' Patsy told him, and the donkey happily followed when she slipped his head collar on and opened the gate.

Buzz was quite happy to be saddled and Katy thought it worth trying. Tomos was delighted. The little stirrups were short enough to accommodate his legs and the child strap across the pommel of the saddle gave a safe hold for small hands. With Buzz walking cheerfully beside her on a short leading rein Patsy set off down the fields to her son in law, Gareth's, family farm.

The horses watched them go. From the field he shared by day with Golly Patsy's Welsh Cob stallion, Heddfa Aur, known as Fly at home, gave an inquiring shriek and his mother, Authin Aur, home name Goldie, came to the fence of her field with Osbourne and Lad, all of them clearly surprised to see Buzz in a different guise. The spring sun was bright on the golden coats of the two cobs, in keeping with their shared Welsh name for gold, and Patsy felt her usual warm pride in them.

There was a path down to the farm across the fields which Patsy had recently bought from Gareth's father, John. It still felt strange to Patsy to realise that this land was now hers. New gates had been added by Gareth and Mack when the purchase went through and in one of these the other horses came to meet them. Horses had accumulated steadily since Patsy had first come to Bryn Uchaf with just her two old faithfuls and the extra land was very welcome. There were now West Wind and her daughter Summer Breeze, at livery because of their nurse owner's work following the COVID crisis, the rescued pony, skewbald Boy, and the two youngsters, Smokey Star and Lucky, Goldie's grey son and her foster foal.

Buzz greeted them with a friendly bray which made Tomos, perched on his back, giggle, and Patsy nodded an acknowledgement to the shade of old wise woman Mary as they passed the peaceful remains of her cottage at the top of the woods.

Closer to the farm they could hear the sound of sheep and also hammering from where work was under way on the second of two new holiday cottages. These were set to provide a new income for John and Rhianne and allow them to stay in the family home without relying on the large flock of sheep which had been starting to be too much for them. Katy's husband Gareth had not wanted to take on the old commercial plod and the endless work of full-time sheep farming which were his parents' lot. It was an unexpected windfall, courtesy of a surprising job for Muff, which had enabled Patsy to help out by buying some more land from John. It had proved a tactful way of helping them to finance the change as well as helping her own horse commitments.

John and Gareth were in a sheep pen in the yard with the recently bought little flock of rare breed sheep which had started to replace the main commercial

flock. They were attractive animals with thick curly fawn fleeces and brown markings on their heads and legs, in increasing demand to rare breed enthusiasts and for their unusual wool. John, a quiet, reserved man with greying brown hair and the tough build of a Welsh farmer, was putting ear tags on them while Gareth, a younger, darker haired and good-looking version of his father, held a protesting ewe. Gareth's mother, Rhianne, dark haired and energetic, turned to see who was coming and laughed, coming with her arms out to meet them and to embrace her grandson.
'Well, and look at you now,' she said. 'Riding in here like a real cowboy. That's a great baby carriage you have there Patsy.'
'It certainly beats pushing that buggy,' Patsy told her.
Rhianne lifted Tomos down and the young brown brindled sheepdog, Bran, who always considered herself his guardian when he was there, came to lie guardian sheepdog fashion with her nose on her front paws and wagged her tail at him. They were watched from the short row of kennels by the three young collies who were part of Gareth's other new venture into sheep dog training, something else which the cutting back on the sheep had allowed him time for. He had always enjoyed it, as did his father, and well-trained young dogs were worth considerable money.
There was a crash and a shout from the direction of the cottage building site and Rhianne looked alarmed. 'That sounded serious,' she said, and she was proved right a few moments later when Ethan, the boy who worked for them and who had been helping the

workmen, hurried round the corner into the yard looking alarmed.

'What is It?' Rhianne asked him, and Ethan said 'Gethin. He was fixing some of that roof guttering that keeps coming loose and the ladder slipped. He looks bad. Can you come and see?'

'That cottage, one thing after another,' exclaimed Rhianne. 'I'm coming, you stay with Nanna Patsy Tomos.'

Tomos was clinging to her leg, looking scared by the sudden sense of crisis, and Patsy said, 'I'll go, here Ethan, take Buzz.'

Ethan and the donkey were old friends, Ethan having worked for the donkey's previous owner before the Covid pandemic had claimed him, and looking relieved now he took charge of Buzz while Patsy went to investigate.

There had been a number of setbacks with this second conversion. The building had been an old longhouse a little apart from the main farm, long and low in the style of the old Pembrokeshire all-purpose buildings. Once it had housed both humans and animals in different sections but more recently it had been used for storage and as a sheep shelter. Now it was being re-built using the original stone, its small windows were being replaced and the original sagging roof was also being replaced with smart, and expensive, new slates. A section of the new guttering was hanging down and there was a man lying on the ground beside a fallen ladder, Gethin, the builder.

'Can't move,' he told Patsy weakly. 'My leg…think it

might be broken...'

By the odd shape of it Patsy thought he might be right. He closed his eyes, looking sick, and Patsy pulled a nearby tool bag over for him to lean on as Gareth came round the corner.

I'll get the jeep,' he said. 'An ambulance could be hours coming. You O.K. with that Gethin, if we can get you in?'

Gethin nodded weakly and Patsy stayed with him until Gareth came back in the farm pick up. It was a painful business but at last Gethin was in the back surrounded by rugs and pillows with the canvas roof in place over him and Gareth beside him and John got in to drive. Rhianne had stayed in the yard with Tomos while Ethan put the sheep back into the barn where they were awaiting imminently due lambs, and Buzz was enjoying a pile of hay.

Turning to go to join them Patsy glanced at the future holiday cottage. It looked somehow cold in spite of the sunshine, and shut off, the new windows blank almost as if it was rejecting her look and for a moment she felt cold herself. It was hard to imagine it welcoming a cheerful family of holiday makers but then this was hardly a good moment to assess it. She went on to find Rhianne and her grandson and to go into the cheerful farm kitchen with them and Ethan to drink coffee and

assess the effect that the accident might have on the future plan.

'It could certainly be holding us up,' Rhianne put fragrant mugs of coffee in front of them and sat down while Ethan found one of Tomos's trucks and began to play with him. 'It wasn't easy finding someone to work on that old place, has to be done careful to match the conservation rules about that old stone, and those that have taken it on have had nothing but trouble. Gethin wasn't keen to take it on but John persuaded him. Makes me feel guilty now this has happened. There's still a deal to do as well, inside's hardly started.'

'Have you put the first one up for renting yet?' Patsy asked and Rhianne nodded.

'With that online booking service,' she said. 'And on the local holiday renting page. Open at Easter. We've got the pod as well, down the field, put that back on now things have opened up again, so it's not all bad news.'

'Is John happy about the sheep?' Patsy knew changing from the traditional farming had been a wrench for him.

'Now he's used to it,' Rhianne laughed. 'He says needing looks more than weight in the stock seems odd value but he likes the new stock, good to handle and sensible with Gareth's young dogs, not panicky about them like some. He's better in himself with a bit less of the work and with Gareth interested again. They're looking forward to the new lambs, nice way to start off the new flock if they should breed a champion.'

"That John was better for the change was the main thing," thought Patsy. John had been diagnosed with angina which had forced his decision to change away from the demands of full-scale sheep farming. She was thankful that things seemed to be moving the right way. The last thing she had wanted was to lose John and Rhianne as neighbours if they were forced to go into a smaller property. As well as losing Rhianne's company she might then find some disruptive new type of farming starting up next door. Muff's unexpected success as dancing mule in a video which had gone viral had proved a lifeline for them all. Tomos was settled for the morning with Rhianne and Ethan agreed to keep an eye on Buzz, who could go in the old orchard, and to walk home with Tomos on him again in time for lunch. Patsy set off for home leaving Tomos playing with Bran on guard and Ethan sorting out the penned sheep.

Rhianne had promised to let her know as soon as there was news of Gethin.

Forrest was there when she got back, brushing Nell in the field with Muff dozing nearby. Forrest was sixteen, a rather skinny boy with brown hair in a tight, high top knot. His family had recently found a new place to settle in a developing eco village where they could develop his mother's insistence on following a more environmentally friendly lifestyle. It was he who had rescued the then in foal mare from an abusive home.

The one-eyed pony was enjoying the attention, leaning into the brush and wrinkling her lips. Patsy told Forrest about the morning's escape.

'She gets worried if she can't wander.' Forrest scratched the mare's neck and she turned the blind side of her head confidently to rub her nose on him.

'She remembers that tether and that old man who had her coming and hurting her. She'd have been happy to work if he hadn't been so rough with her.'

'It's a shame she's not a bit bigger so that you could ride her.' Patsy looked at the pony. She was about thirteen two and Forrest did sometimes step onto her bareback but his feet did hang very near the ground. 'What about driving her? You said her last owner tried to use her to pull a harrow.'

'He scared her,' said Forrest. 'She wanted to look round to see where she was and he got mad with her.'

'We could try starting her again,' Patsy suggested.

'She gets bored and restless now Muff's got independent. We could start long reining her but try bridling her first. My old pony's tack should fit.'

It seemed a long time since David, one of the two original horses she had brought to Wales with her, had died, but his tack had been kept dry and oiled and he had been about the same size as Nell.

The grey pony had obviously been bitted before but not too comfortably. She opened her mouth rather too wide and then champed on it, tossing her head up and down, and Patsy asked Forrest what the last bit had been.

'A long bar,' Forrest sounded doubtful. 'With sort of long strips at the end with holes in them for the reins. And there were pads on the head thing over her eyes.'

It sounded like an old driving bridle. Nell must have felt almost blind with blinkers over her eyes when she only had half sight anyway.

'She should be more comfortable in this,' she told

Forrest. She found a second lunge rein and clipped them both onto the rings of the snaffle bit and showed Forrest how to hold them before leading Nell into the school. "No whip," she decided. "Better to try without one if the pony had been frightened by one."

She led Nell round once, feeling her tense beside her, then stepped back and told Forrest to walk on behind the pony.

'Talk to her,' she said. 'Let her know you're the person driving her.'

It seemed to work. Nell was jumpy at first, going in fits and starts with her ears turned back and once turning her whole head to check who was behind her, but gradually she relaxed and it was obvious that she had done this before. There was definite understanding between her and the boy walking behind and Patsy knew that she was watching something quite unusual. Forrest had rescued her and she clearly remembered and trusted him now. After a few circuits and a change of direction Forrest pulled up, grinning.

'She didn't go like that when the old man was driving her, 'he said. 'It were all shouting and slapping at her.'

'She trusts you,' Patsy told him. 'You could take her round the fields like that, give her something different to do.'

Forrest liked the idea and Nell, turning to nuzzle him, looked as though she agreed.

Ethan brought Buzz and Tomos back at lunch time as he had promised and reported that Gethin had indeed broken his leg.

'He's going to be off for weeks,' he told Patsy. 'Me and Gareth can fix bits of it but there's the roof to finish, that's specialist work, one of those windows isn't right, and there's all the fitting inside.'

Patsy knew that it was not going to be easy. Most experienced local workmen were booked for months ahead and there was a limit to what anyone inexperienced could do.

Tomos did not want to get off Buzz.

'You've started something there,' said Mack, as he watched Katy detaching a reluctant small boy from the donkey's saddle. 'I can see us all being in for a spot of walking.'

'Your idea Mum,' Katy set her son down on his feet. 'Buzz wants his lunch now, Tomos, and it's time for yours.'

She led Tomos firmly away and Mack laughed.

'I remember donkey rides on Brighton beach as a small boy,' he said. 'Kids never change, donkey rides and ice cream. Seems a long time ago.'

'You still like riding,' Patsy reminded him.

'Talking of which,' Mack turned towards the barn. 'I could do with a blast...how about a gallop and a late lunch?'

Half an hour later, sitting on Golly high on the Preselis beside Mack on his big old horse, Patsy knew that it was a good idea. The sweet air was warm on her face, lower down the moor was flushed with the first green, the gorse bushes blazed with golden flower and a skylark was singing as it spiralled into the shining endless blue of the spring sky. Beside her Mack was windblown and happy from the gallop up from the causeway, still showing the inheritance of that donkey riding boy he had once been, and Patsy felt her own years fall away as he grinned at her.

'Come on,' he said. 'Switchback way down and Osbourne will beat you to the gate.'

Knowing what she was in for Patsy laughed back at him and shortened her reins. Mack merely moved his heels against his horse's sides and Osbourne was off straight into a canter on Mack's usual loose rein, along the top of the still brown bracken thicket and round into the steep, irregular downhill path. This was worn into ridges and sharp drops by water and the coming and going of the wild ponies and both horses, familiar with it, went down sitting back with their hocks well under them, sending showers of small stones and clumps of mud down with them. A rabbit shot out of their way and a buzzard swooped low overhead hoping for easy prey. As the path levelled out along more even going Mack sent Osbourne forging ahead and Patsy leaned forward to urge Golly after him. They came onto the smoother green causeway neck and neck and as the gate drew closer Osbourne's long neck kept him a nose in front. Then Patsy, a fraction more cautious, began to pull up and they arrived at a trot as Osbourne skidded to a last second stop with his nose almost touching the gate.

'Wimp,' Mack was laughing at her, and Patsy said 'Wimp yourself, I reckon you just couldn't stop.

Look at us, what are we like, in our dotage and fooling about like teenagers.'

'Why should teenagers have all the fun?' Mack leaned down from his bigger horse to grab her shoulder and pull her over for a kiss as the horses churned about excitedly in front of the gate.

'Do you know Mrs. Macintosh, I really do fancy you. That's something else teenagers don't have sole rights over.'

As he let her go and turned Osbourne to open the gate Patsy enjoyed the shared knowledge that he was right. It still seemed odd to ride past the gate to Mack's house and not be met by the donkeys but since the COVID threat had died down Mack's ex-wife Tabitha, with her new husband Flynn and stepdaughter Summer, had moved back to London. Mack had now let the house to a doctor who wanted to see if he and his family liked living in the slower rhythm of life in Pembrokeshire. The grass in the paddock was long and still winter yellow and the shelter from which gentle Harley had gone to cross the rainbow bridge had spider's webs across it. Their horses paused automatically at the gate, still half expecting the donkeys to be there to meet them.

Patsy had received a text from Summer saying that she missed them and the horses. Flynn was doubtful now about her having her own horse as he said she would soon be going to uni.

'I'm not even sure I want to go,' she had written. 'But Dad seems to take it for granted that I will.'

She also said that she missed the people she had come to know although she was glad to see her old friends again. Patsy suspected that one of the people she was missing was Ethan, with whom she had grown close through their joint fondness for the donkeys.

Flynn and Tabitha had found a house they liked in Surrey, on a good rail link to London for Flynn's theatre work, and there were livery stables in the area. It would be a good area for riding but Patsy could understand Flynn's doubts about buying her a horse although he had promised to do so.

Mack patted Osbourne's neck, looking across the empty paddock towards his old house.

'We had some fights in there, me and Tabs,' he said. 'I hope she's more peaceful with Flynn. It didn't really work for us but we just wanted different things.'

'No regrets?' Patsy risked asking, and when Mack turned his head to smile at her she knew the answer.

'None,' he said softly. 'Come on, let's get home and I'll prove it.'

Back at Bryn Uchaf the donkeys came to the fence to meet them and Patsy realised that it was well past lunch time.

'Hot rolls and cheese?' she suggested as they turned the horses out, and Mack hugged her.

'Sounds good,' he said. 'And then there's something else good to follow.'

Agreeing Patsy told herself that it might seem ridiculous to feel as she did at that reminder. She and Mack were far from being teenagers but what they shared was as young and warm as it would ever have been and she felt a delicious stir of anticipation at the prospect. They headed into the house with arms round each other and had to be firm with themselves to remember that lunch should really come first.

CHAPTER TWO

Two days later Rhianne reported several bookings for the completed cottage and the pod.

'It seems there's a good demand out there,' she said. 'The chance of riding is getting interest as well, one inquiry asked if they could bring their own horses and others want to hire.'

Visiting horses was an interesting idea. Katy thought so too.

'So long as they're grass kept,' she said. 'We've plenty of grazing now with those extra fields. There's that strip of grass by the young horses, they could go in there and come in the stable here to tack up. They'd need a guide out on the hill though.'

'Jobs for us,' Patsy told her. 'Anything to get this holiday business going. I'll tell Rhianne to say yes. I'd better see if I can borrow Cinder and Sweep again if there's really going to be a demand for riding. '

Cinder and Sweep had proved useful for visiting riders in the past. Their owner, a lively lady who taught aerobics and ran her own clinics, had little time to ride and she had been glad to have them exercised now that her daughter had left home. She was pleased with the prospect of them having some work and Patsy agreed that she would collect them.

There had been no success yet in finding another workman with time to take on the work on the new cottage. There had been a series of unlucky setbacks, a new wall collapsing, specially made window frames which proved not to fit, a breaking sheet of glass which had cut a workman's arm badly enough to need stitching. Originally the new cottage had been planned to be a conversion of part of the old cow sheds but that would have meant losing a useful part of the main yard and John had been persuaded to use this site instead.

'I think he'd have been better doing it his way,' was Katy's comment. 'That old store's always seemed a bit spooky to me, sort of unfriendly out on its own in that bit of rough ground. It's a damp spot too, Gareth says hay never kept well in it and some calves he tried to raise in there got pneumonia. He wishes now that he hadn't talked John into using it, but he said it made commercial sense to use something that was no use as it was.'

Patsy remembered her own uncomfortable feeling about the building but it had been neglected for a long time, it would be fine when it was finished, furnished, and cheerfully occupied she told herself firmly.

Patsy and Katy went to collect the trekking ponies next day. Cinders and Sweep were cobs, Welsh crosses not the hotter Welsh pure-bred cobs. They we're still shaggy with their winter coats. Mack looked at them doubtfully when they came out of the old horse box.

'A bit of work for you here,' he said to Patsy. 'Sure you

want it? Rhianne doesn't have to offer riding.'

'I can do with a project,' Patsy told him. 'And anything to give this cottage business an extra boost. It's going to be slower getting going anyway with this building holdup. And a good excuse for more riding. You can come out as well.'

'Pony trekking isn't quite Osbourne's thing,' said Mack, but Patsy knew that he would be happy to try it out. He always welcomed any time spent on his beloved Preseli hills.

There were other horse changes coming as well. The owner of Patsy's two livery horses would soon be coming to collect them now that the Covid crisis had eased and she was planning to take them home now that she could cut back on her work as a nurse and return to semi-retirement.

'That will leave me without a regular horse to ride,' said Katy. 'Fly will soon be back to covering mares and Goldie's in foal. I remember Cinders can be quite a decent ride if she's woken up but I can't escort on her if she's needed for riders.'

'There's Boy,' Patsy reminded her. 'He's too young for anyone inexperienced.'

'I wish Smokey was grown up,' Katy sounded impatient. 'He's three now, he could at least be backed All these horses here and half of them are young or busy breeding.'

Patsy supposed that she was right but she did not want to rush him. Smokey Star had been bred with great plans in mind for him as Katy's serious competition horse. It would be stupid to take any risks with his still developing bones.

After some tidying up and a lunging session for each of them Patsy suggested a gentle ride to remind the ponies of their job. She would ride Sweep herself and Katy could ride the sharper Cinder. Mack announced that he would come with them on Osbourne. Katy, who had experienced Mack's idea of a gentle ride before, grinned.

'I hope you can control him Mum, 'she said. 'Him and that old horse have never gone for a quiet ride in their lives. He'll be giving the cobs the wrong idea. You'd be better leaving him babysitting, Gareth says taking Tomos to Rhianne with him now means Buzz has to go as well.'

She had certainly started something there, Patsy knew. Going to his other Grandmother now included taking the donkey as Tomos refused to go quietly without him. Buzz was quite happy about this, he liked attention and a chance of foraging in the different patches of rough grazing round the farm. Gareth did report one oddity, however.

'He's picky about the patches he likes,' he told Patsy, when he brought Buzz and his passenger back later. 'I put him in that old patch round the new cottage, there's some soft young thistles coming through, but he wouldn't stay, came looking for us round by the sheep, he did. I remember Dad saying the sheep never grazed much there when it was all one field. The dogs are a bit wary too.'

"The cottage again", Patsy felt a prickle of un-ease. There couldn't really be anything disturbing about the new holiday home, surely.

Cinder and Sweep seemed happy to be back on the moor with Mack in the lead on his big skewbald.

It was a day of sharp showers and fast-moving clouds so that brilliant patches of sunlight swept across the heathery ground, a day made for fast canters between the thickets of gorse, but the ponies were unfit although Osbourne soon became impatient.

'Oh, let him have a run,' said Katy, as Osbourne shook his head impatiently and even made Mack shorten his reins for once. 'I don't think these two will be bothered.'

Mack took her at her word. He let Osbourne have his usual long rein and went off across a stretch of sheep bitten grass in a plunging gallop. The two cobs, secure in each other's familiar company, jogged a few steps and then subsided. Katy laughed.

'He'd really miss that old horse,' she said to Patsy. 'I wonder if Mack's always ridden like that.'

'Yes,' said Patsy. 'He rides for the feeling of freedom and the transport on the hills. So long as his horse is happy to go anywhere he wants out there it's all he asks. He can manage Lad well enough but he likes his horse to find its own going, not rely on him.'

Mack was turning Osbourne back towards them now, the horse choosing his own route between the gorse bushes and neatly avoiding a boggy patch, and Patsy knew that Katy was right. If something happened to his familiar old horse Mack would certainly find it hard to replace him. They were like Forrest and Nell, she realised, a close understanding that bridged the gap between human and animal minds. It was a gift that not every rider was lucky enough to know although she felt close to it with her own skewbald Golly.

It seemed like foresight when, two days later, Osbourne was lame. They were setting out on another ride with the cobs, Patsy riding Cinder and leading Sweep as they needed to get fitter and Katy had to work. They started to trot on the lane which led up to the green road, the old track which crossed the high farmland a little lower than the Golden Road, and Mack said, 'This doesn't feel quite right. Will you watch him.'

He sent Osbourne into the lead and Patsy saw it at once.

'He's not quite sound behind,' she said. 'Perhaps he's picked up a stone.'

Mack got off to look, Osbourne standing loose while he had his hind feet picked up, but Mack reported nothing there.

'It might wear off,' Patsy was hopeful. 'It's probably a bruise, we'd better walk and take the short way back.'

Osbourne did not seem worried, he was sound walking and when they got home his legs felt cool and there were no obvious swellings.

'I'll give him a couple of days off and see what happens.' Mack patted his old horse and Osbourne felt hopefully round his pockets. 'Let's hope you're right and he's trodden on a sharp stone.'

Forrest had proved to be there when they got back, brushing a rather surprised Muff while her mother looked on with a benign expression on her face.

'She was looking for Buzz,' explained Forrest. 'Soon as I tried to take Nell for a walk she started trying to get out the way he'd gone.'

Patsy knew that he was right. Buzz meant more security to the little mule than her renegade mother did.

'Is something up with that horse?' Forrest had been watching them examine Osbourne and Patsy explained.

'My Mum might help,' Forrest told her. 'She's good with herbs and such when anyone hurts themselves or has a cold.'

'Is she?' Patsy was interested. 'We'll see how it goes but I won't forget. Shouldn't you be at school by the way?' Forrest shook his head.

'I've left,' he told her. 'I'm old enough now and I wasn't up to much at learning. I do a few jobs round about.'

'What about your sisters?' Patsy asked him and Forrest said, 'Leaf's older than me, she's left as well, works in Mum's herb and green produce garden. Brooke's younger, Mum still has to send her to school or there'd be trouble. Brooke hates school, she gets teased a lot because we live different

although she's quite good at the work. Likes reading and such but really she just wants to be with animals, she's mad on horses, she loved Nell when we were stopped at the old man's place.'

'Are you looking for work?' Patsy thought of the cottage. There were plenty of jobs still to do before it was ready for use and not all of them were skilled. Any help with it would be welcomed.

'With horses?' Forrest sounded keen but Patsy explained and his face fell.

'I suppose I could do a bit,' he admitted. 'Though I'm helping Dad build our round house at the eco place right now. Stones and turf and that'.

Patsy decided to suggest it to Gareth. At the moment work on the cottages seemed to be taking up as much of his time as the sheep had been and his work at home as an I.T. consultant like Katy, was suffering although he was happy to cut down on it a bit now that his sheep dogs were starting to pay.

Osbourne was still not quite sound three days later and Mack got the farrier to look at his feet.

'Nothing there that he could find, 'he told Patsy, afterwards, I suppose I'd better get the vet to have a look.'

Patsy knew that he was reluctant to do this in case the diagnosis was bad but Osbourne was still not sound and as they feared it was depressing news.

'But of arthritis in that hock,' said the vet. 'I can try injections but it's there's no guarantee they will work. It's age related, of course. Over twenty, isn't he? We'll try putting him on a spot of Bute first. Give him a week off and see how it goes.'

It was depressing news and Patsy knew that they would both feel it. Osbourne had always seemed a defining part of Mack, from the first moment she had seen him when he stopped a loose David from going off with some wild ponies. It was still the way he lived now, riding his old horse freely over the hills, shaking off hints of his own increasing age and immersing himself in his love of the wild country. She imagined Mack slowing up, losing the still youthful edge which was one of the things she loved in him. It would affect her as well, she knew.

'Bute,' said Mack, after the vet had gone. 'Possible damage to his digestion and the danger of him not feeling some injury until it gets serious. And probably everything a bit blunted like we feel on paracetamol. Is it better like that so that he can work for my benefit or would he be better staying in the field and feeling a bit stiff. I know which I'd choose.'

'You could try the injections if it doesn't work,' Patsy pointed out, but she knew that there were reports of that treatment making things worse. As for the effect of Bute ....

'He's a horse,' she reminded Mack. 'He doesn't think like you. He doesn't rely on the images in his head like we do to keep him fulfilled. He just wants to be comfortable.'

'How do you know?' Mack was not convinced. 'He may have all sorts of things going on in his head that we can't imagine, Images and senses different to ours. I might be blunting all that.'

Even while he was talking Osbourne suddenly raised his head, ears pricked and staring away down the field, and they both saw the brown flicker of a fox slipping under the hedge.

'Like that, 'said Mack, 'Terrific senses of hearing, sight, and probably more.'

'But Bute isn't just a pain killer,' Patsy reminded him.

'Ee an anti-inflammatory as well. Give it a chance. At least you can ride Lad.'
But she knew that Mack was not convinced although he said that he would try using it.
Forrest said his Dad thought doing some work on the cottage would be good for him.
'He's happy to go along with the way Mum wants to live but he doesn't want me thinking it's the only way,' he told Patsy.
'Sounds like a sensible man,' said Mack, when he heard, and Patsy agreed.
John was happy to take on even unskilled help and Gareth said that with an extra pair of hands they could get on with putting in some of the inside fittings.
The first visitors were due at the completed cottage which was close to the main house and which had once been a stable. The conversion of this one had been straight forward and it looked homely and welcoming with a small, securely fenced garden safe for children and small dogs to run in. Rhianne had decided to allow dogs but stated in her advertisement that they must not be allowed a chance to run loose. Now that the start was so close she was getting nervous.
'There's no knowing they'll like it,' she said. 'There, we could be putting all of this planning into something that might not work.'
'Your pod visitors have always been happy,' Patsy reminded her, as Rhianne took her for a final look round. 'I know they're mainly people for the walking

and this is more for families but this is great, cosy and pretty and with that great view over to the hills. It'll be fine.'

But she knew that Rhianne could not help worrying. Their being able to keep the farm depended so much on the success of the cottages.

There was one instant success. The visitors arrived just as Patsy and Buzz were collecting Tomos from a morning with Rhianne. There were shrieks of delight, hastily hushed, from the two little girls in the family at the sight of the donkey who pricked his ears towards them with obvious welcome.

'Can we ride on him?' The bigger girl was stroking Buzz and Patsy knew that she was cornered. It seemed that Buzz's days of giving rides were not over. She agreed to bring him in the morning and the girl's mother promised to have a supply of carrots waiting.

'It'll be the making of our holiday for them,' she told Patsy. 'My husband likes to walk but his walks are often too ambitious for the girls and I have trouble finding things to keep them entertained. If they can look forward to donkey rides it will help.'

Patsy promised to bring Buzz over each day and when the children had gone Rhianne looked relieved.

'I was trying to think of things for them,' she told Patsy. 'Their Dad wanting his long walks sounded a bit selfish but their Mum was telling me he's getting over a breakdown and walking has been suggested to help him.'

'Buzz is in demand anyway with his buggy job,' Patsy told her. 'I think he's enjoying being useful again.'

Forrest's father brought him over to start work next day and he was immediately interested in the building. He was a stocky, fair-haired man with close cropped hair, not in the least Patsy's imaginary picture of someone with ideas of an alternative green lifestyle. He had driven over in a well-used camper van with a useful looking selection of builders' ladders and tools on a trailer behind. He surveyed the partly restored cottage with professional interest and remarked that some of the stonework was a bit rough. 'You'll be getting damp in round those back windows,' he told Patsy, who was there as promised with Buzz. 'And that corner stone could do with re-setting.'
'Dad's a stone mason,' Forrest explained, and Patsy looked at him with fresh interest. The building work had been rather scrambled, she knew, and something about the whole effect was not quite right.
'Is it too late to improve it?' she asked and Mr. Higgins, call me Al, ran a hand thoughtfully down the stone.
'Shouldn't take too much,' he said. 'But there's something strikes me as not quite right. I'd have to see.'
'Would you take on the job of putting it right?' Patsy asked him, and Al said that he should be able to fit it in.
'Almost got our Hobbit house to Ana's liking,' he said. 'Tidy little job of turfs and stone. It all needs to settle a bit now.'
'Alright for us to carry on inside?' asked Gareth, and Al shrugged.
'Shouldn't cause any problems,' he said.' Probably just

a matter of chipping and filling. I'll come back with the boy tomorrow, when I've tidied up a few bits back at our place.'

The little girls were out now clamouring for a ride and Patsy turned to deal with them leaving Forrest's father still looking thoughtfully at the cottage.

Buzz seemed quite happy back in his job of giving rides. He walked up and down the farm drive wearing his benign expression while Rhianne distracted Tomos who plainly thought that the donkey was his property.

'Tomorrow?' begged the girls and Patsy had to agree. It looked as if this first family of visitors anyway were having a holiday that they would remember.

'But my next lot are expecting something bigger,' Rhianne warned Patsy, who returned home thinking that Sweep and Cinders needed another outing.

Mack came out while she was saddling the ponies and looked regretfully at Osbourne, still having his advised break in the field before starting on the slower regime advised for him.

'Come with us on Lad,' Patsy told him and Mack decided that he would.

Katy was working and so Patsy rode the grey cob and led Sweep. It seemed strange to see Mack on the lightly built bay thoroughbred instead of the skewbald who seemed, when out on the moor, to be almost his alter ego. He had to sit differently on Lad, keeping his heels well away from the sensitive sides and keeping his hands light but firm on the reins. It was not his way. Riding Osbourne set him free, exercise and transport through the wild country while his mind was free for plots and characters for his books to develop. Lad was straight forward and, for an ex-racehorse, sensible, but he did expect conventional aids and constant light control. There were some things about riding him, however, that Mack did enjoy. Leaving Patsy trotting the two cobs steadily along the flat, he turned Lad up the Haffod track and sent him forward into his smooth, fast, long striding thoroughbred gallop and came back looking exhilarated with Lad bright and relaxed.

'Alright,' he said to Patsy, when she grinned at him. 'Maybe there are some perks to riding a speed merchant.'

He patted Lad, who pricked his ears and jogged, suggesting he could enjoy more of that, but Patsy knew that riding him was not really the answer that Mack wanted.

Katy was riding herself when they got back, seizing the chance between online jobs while Tomos was with Rhianne. She had Fly in the school, all arched neck and big cob trot as he showed off to the unimpressed Nell, Muff, and Jack over the fence. She had music playing on her device on the school mounting block, a bouncy arranged disk made for her by Mack's ex-wife's new musician husband Flynn. He had become a keen arranger of music for free style dressage while living close by in Mack's house which had at the time still been partly owned by Tabitha.

Watching them while she unsaddled the cobs and Mack dealt with Lad Patsy could see that free style really suited the showy cob stallion. Fly was usually too busy with visiting mares to compete much in the spring but perhaps, now that shows were coming back into full swing after the COVID break it might be time to re-think his schedule.

'There's a dressage day with a music test at that indoor centre near Haverfordwest,' Katy told her later. 'I could see what he makes if it. He hasn't got a mare booked for a bit yet.'

'I could bring Boy,' Flynn had made a disc for Patsy and the young skewbald rescue pony as well. 'I enjoyed doing a bit of competing again last year. But you'd better check that they don't mind stallions at the show and make sure Gareth or Rhianne can have Tomos.'

Rhianne was quite happy about that and Katy sent in the entries and started to chivvy her mother into regular schooling sessions. Watching one of these Mack shook his head.

'I can see the attraction of riding to music,' he said. 'But this going in circles and counting strides wouldn't do it for me. Horses are for freedom, not fiddling about in enclosures.'

'There's room for both,' Patsy told him. 'I wouldn't want to school all the time but it is satisfying getting that feel of harmony and lightness that you can share with a schooled horse, and teaching them to achieve it.'

'Each to his own,' said Mack, but Patsy knew that he was not convinced.

CHAPTER THREE

Al Higgins came back as promised and set to work tidying the stonework while Forrest worked inside the cottage with Ethan and Gareth, who both took turns between farm work and fitting out the interior. It was not going easily. There were frequent problems with screws and nails which refused to hold and with measurements which proved to be out. John said that they should have converted the old cowshed instead as he had wanted.

'Always been a frowsty old building,' he said. 'Would have been better left alone. My Da, he wouldn't let me and my brother play there, he was right after what happened to Eirig.'

'What was that?' Pasty asked him. She was there with Buzz, collecting Tomos. John stroked the donkey's ears and looked at her.

'Used to be an old half floor in there, see,' he said. 'We were climbing up to it, that old ladder broke and Eirig, he fell off, hit his head. Never quite the same, he wasn't, after that. Wasn't the first accident there either, my Nannie, she'd fallen down in there and broke her hip, brought on the stroke she died from, though fair enough, she was in her eighties, but he blamed that old building, said it was only good for storage after.'

Patsy stared at him, startled, but then Tomos arrived, demanding to get onto Buzz, and John picked him up and set him on the donkey's back before turning away. Rhianne shook her head and when John had headed towards the sheep pen she said, 'He doesn't like talking much about his brother. Dead a while now, died in that care home he'd been living in for years. Their Mum, she always blamed John, him being older, for encouraging his brother to go climbing in there.'

No wonder John would have preferred the other site for the cottage, thought Patsy. She wondered if Gareth knew this story.

'Uncle Eirig,' said Gareth.,' when Patsy asked him. 'I never met him, Da didn't like him mentioned much. I knew there was some shadow over him. He died when I was about six. If I had known I'd not have been pushing Da so much about the site but it seemed sense. Started as a cottage anyway, farm hands used to live in it along with some stock. Places holding memories like that might be best left in peace.'

But that was just superstition. Old buildings must always hold memories, good and bad, thought Patsy, but she could not help a feeling of unease.

When he finished work each day Forrest spent some time with Nell, driving her in the long reins or taking her for walks on which he would step on and ride her for short distances. He was not heavy but his long legs did hang a long way below her tummy. The little mare was more peaceful now that she had these outings and Muff was quite happy left with the donkeys.

The little mule was a great character, curious about everything and quick to learn. Anything left in reach from feed bowls to a carelessly left garment on the fence was carried off, examined, and turned into a plaything. She encouraged Buzz to play tug of war and to toss things about and chase them and one morning Patsy saw both Muff and the donkey with sticks in their mouths waving them at one another as if they were fencing.

'Shame you didn't have a camera,' said Katy, when Patsy described the scene. 'You could have made another video, it might have made money like the one Flynn made of her already has.'

'It was his music with it that really caught on,' Patsy reminded her. 'I saw his name in Radio Times, he's choreographer for that new dance series that's being made.'

'Gareth said Ethan had a text from Summer the other day,' Katy told her. 'She did sound a bit down. They're in the new house now but Flynn still keeps on about uni and not the right time to have a horse. He's given her driving lessons for her seventeenth birthday instead but she reckons he'd have wanted her to learn to drive anyway.'

Patsy thought this was probably true. One thing she suspected, however. It wasn't just a horse that Summer was missing.

'She was quite keen on Ethan wasn't she,' Patsy said, and Katy agreed.

'I don't think she's had any other boyfriends,' she said.

'I think Tabitha makes sure they keep her on a pretty tight rein.'

Remembering Mack's ex-wife Patsy knew that Katy was right but Summer had been a feisty sort of girl. She would not accept unwanted restrictions for ever.

The day of the dressage event arrived. Stallions could take part but had to wear a stallion disc on their bridle. 'Not that there'll be much doubt if he gives his usual display,' said Mack dryly as he watched them load, the gleaming, curvy chestnut, all prance and energy and the calm, plain skewbald. 'Got your music?'

Patsy made a final check in the dashboard drawer and assured him that they had. Mack was not coming to spectate as he had a deadline to meet for an article on thriller writing for which was commissioned.

It was a bright but showery day with a gusty wind sending the showers rattling fast across the fields but the show was being held at a local equitation centre with good parking and warm up area as well as a roomy indoor school. To Fly shows normally meant either being led in hand or trotting and cantering round with a group of horses. Dressage, working separately and entering the ring alone, was a new experience. To Boy it was more familiar. The warmup was in the outdoor arena among other horses and while Boy remained quite calm about it Fly was in full show mode, all arched neck and high steps with pricked ears and throaty murmurs as he passed a tasty mare. The other riders eyed him anxiously, those riding mares gave him a wide berth and there were sighs of relief when his number was called.

Fly was not impressed by the indoor school. He had been enjoying showing off outside and this quiet indoor space with its air of concentration was claustrophobic. He was tense and distracted, looking at the door and shying at his reflection in the mirrors on the wall and Patsy could hear him shouting for company. They came bounding out with Katy looking hot and frazzled and the stallion sweating and snatching at his bit. He greeted open space and other horses with a shout of relief and Katy swung him in a circle before getting off.

'Did he actually do the test?' Patsy asked her and Katy said 'Sort of. He just didn't see the point. I just hope he'll settle down in the freestyle.'

Both horses were entered for the prelim test first and Boy's number was being called as Katy led the still excited cob away towards the lorry.

Boy ignored all this excitement. Indoor schools were new to him as well but he was prepared to accept it as another sort of barn and he went calmly through the simple movements. He was naturally in shape with a rounded outline and when they came to a final nicely square halt Patsy felt a pleasant glow of success. Her rough little rescue pony, abandoned as unwanted on the hill, had proved satisfyingly worth-while.

'That was good,' Katy sounded impressed, and the result proved her right when Boy was placed second.

The freestyle tests at different levels were being judged in one group, marked for the level of the compulsory movements set for each test. Fly was a little more settled in the warmup and when he went back into the school and his music started he relaxed. It was familiar after the time Katy had spent practising to it and his reaction was almost automatic, taking him from one pace to the next in time with it. It was lovely to watch, the curvy golden horse with his big paces turning Flynn's clever arrangement into something visual.

There was a scatter of applause from the few spectators and Patsy suspected that Katy had won the class even with a novice standard test. She was right and Katy was thrilled.

'I thought my dressage days would be over soon when Eleri comes to take her ponies home,' she said. 'But maybe Fly can take over until Smokey grows up.'

'I thought Smokey was set to be an eventer,' said Patsy, but Katy pointed out that dressage was part of Eventing anyway. They loaded the horses for a triumphant drive home.

Getting out from the lorry in the yard Patsy was surprised by the deserted feel of it. No Mack coming out to ask how they had got on, no Gareth home with Tomos and Buzz and not many horses watching at the gates.

'Look as if Mack's pinched your horse,' said Katy, and Patsy realised that one of the deserters was Lad. She felt a twinge of resentment. She and Mack had always been careful not to take some things for granted and one of them was respecting one another's horses. Osbourne might be resting at the moment but he could at least have asked her before going off for one of his head clearing hacks.

'What's yours is obviously his as well,' said Katy, who had seen her mother's expression, and then Fly stopped on his way to the stable to stare at the gate and they heard hooves coming down the lane. Mack came into sight leading Lad, who was obviously sore, and Patsy saw blood on his white fetlock

Mack looked wet and mud splashed and unusually ruffled.

'What happened?' Patsy left Boy in his box and went to look as Mack led Lad into his own stable. She was prepared to be cross but Mack said. 'He's got an overreach. We had a bit of drama and I'm afraid I forgot to put his boots on.'

'Drama?' Patsy was bending to look at the horse's foot. There was quite a nasty cut in his front heel where he had trodden on it with a back foot. 'Why? What happened?'

'It was that holiday family at John's,' Mack told her. 'The man whom Rhianne said was recovering from a breakdown. He went off walking first thing and didn't come back. His wife tried to phone him but his phone wasn't working and she got worried. Mass search team out of Gareth and Ethan on quads, John in jeep, and they asked me to come on a horse. Then the chap turns up in a taxi, he'd got lost, come down off the hill at Maenclochog, and got a ride back in a taxi from the local garage.'

'And what happened to Lad?' Patsy thought that she could imagine it, the sense of emergency, fear of a heart attack or collapse. Rhianne would be worried about the threat of disaster in her new cottage business and the search would need a horse to cover the rougher bits of country. Lad's accident would not really have been Mack's fault.

Mack looked guilty. 'I suppose I forgot I wasn't on Osbourne,' he said. 'Came down from the rocks a bit fast on a loose rein and he nearly fell over. I'm really sorry.'

'He'll be off for a bit,' Patsy could not help still feeling cross with him although she knew it was not really his fault. Time could have been important if the man had been in trouble. Mack had taken Lad's tack off and she went to connect the hose. The main problem with an overreach was to keep the flap of skin free from collecting mud.

Buzz had been left at Rhianne's with Tomos while the search went on and Gareth arrived back with both him and his little rider and bringing apologies for the disturbance from the holiday family.

'I told Mam I'd run off some large- scale maps of the hill and mark the safe walks,' he told Patsy. 'She can leave them in the cottages.'

'You need to mark every lump of rock and boggy hole for some people,' said Katy. 'But they'll still get into trouble.'

Patsy knew that this was probably true. The fairly gentle hills were deceptively wild and it was easy to under-estimate them and choose the wrong paths between bog and rocks. She finished hosing Lad's foot and sprayed the cut thoroughly with protective spray and said that she would phone the farrier about the lost shoe.

'It looks as if I'm going to miss my old boy,' said Mack ruefully. 'I'm not tuned in for these fancy creatures that need help controlling their own feet although I admit they give a great feel. I'll probably have to accept that most of us will need a bit of drug therapy as we get older and try him on the vet's powders.'
Although she was still a bit cross Patsy did sympathise with him. She knew how important to him were his rides on his familiar horse.
The farrier, who had know Mack and his horse before Patsy met him, was also understanding.
'Fair play, there aren't many horses who'd be right for Mack's way on them,' he said. 'He's more like a cowboy, those long reins and letting them find their own ways over hills. I'll keep a mind to it if I come to hear of anything that might do his job.'
Rhianne's first lot of visitors finished their holiday and left amid frantic goodbye hugs for Buzz from the little girls. The incoming group included a lady and her daughter who were interested in riding and they had booked two rides in advance.
'Let's both take them,' Patsy told Katy. 'If you ride Boy he'll get some idea of what's needed.'
'And Lad can't go because he's still sore after Rhianne's drama,' said Katy. 'At this rate we're going to have a shortage of horses in work. Maybe we should break Nell in properly, plenty of one-eyed ponies get ridden and she's fine when Forrest sits on her.'
'Why not?' said Patsy. 'She's a bit small but she'd be fine for the lighter riders, or we could ride her and use Boy for clients.'

Nell was quite happy about becoming a riding pony. Long reining had taught her a lot about rein aids and she accepted a saddle with no objection. Forrest stepped onto her and she walked round the school with him as if she had been doing it for ages.

'Now all you have to do is learn to ride so that you can teach her,' Patsy told him. 'You could learn the aids and trotting and cantering on Sweep.'

Forrest was quite happy about it and when he told his sisters he reported that Brooke was jealous.

'She wants to ride, 'he said. 'Leaf told her she's going to turn into a boring pony kid like some of her conventional little school mates but she doesn't care. She's had a few goes on a friend's pony. If Nell learns to do the things most horses do, trotting and things with me riding, could she have a go?'

'Why not?' Patsy thought it a useful idea. It looked as if riding was going to be popular with the cottage visitors.

The first holiday trek was a success. The riders loved the Preselis, their height and space, the magnificent views across green fields and white buildings to the changing colours of the sea, and they were fascinated by the legends and history. There were many, Arthur and Merlin, the stories of the fairy mist which could carry an unwary walker away to fairy land, and the solid history of the

transportation of the bluestones to build Stonehenge.

'It's a magic land isn't it?' commented the mother. 'We'd never heard of it until Liza saw the advertisement for the cottage. Lots of people must be the same.'

'Like Cornwall,' said her daughter. 'Holidays introduced it to so many and now Mum couldn't find anywhere with vacancies and we decided to try here instead. Perhaps it'll get more crowded here as other people do the same.'

Patsy agreed, but with mixed feelings. It would be good business but she remembered the queuing cars and crowded little streets of Cornwall and could not help hoping West Wales would not become quite like that.

Forrest had no trouble learning the basics of riding. He already had his balance from sitting on Nell who seemed just as happy with him as a conventional rider although they both had to learn about rein and leg aids and rising trot. The first time Forrest tried this it startled the pony into a jump forward and a turning of the sighted side of her head to check what was going on. Nell did like her mouth left free enough for her to turn to look at things on her blind side and Patsy decided that it was best to let her do so.

Mack was missing riding. He took to going for long walks over the hills instead and Patsy found herself talked into going with him. Keeping up with Mack's long stride was hard work but there were some advantages to being on foot. There were no distractions from restless horses when they sat down for half an hour to admire a view, time to appreciate the wide spread of the green country and to watch the changing light and the soaring birds. There were other pleasures too, lying back in a sheltered corner sharing a few minutes of quiet affection on the soft spring grass with the strengthening sun warm and the skylarks song raining down on them. In spite of all this Mack did find Osbourne's rest frustrating. He tried riding him out quietly with one of the holiday rides but although he was willing and looked happy to be out he was still not sound.

'You'll have to try Bute unless you retire him,' Patsy told Mack, but they had both heard reports of the bad side effects of the drug and Mack was not happy about it.

'For short term use for injuries yes, and for inflammation but I don't like the idea of long term use.It won't cure him,' he said. 'And long-term use can cause a lot of harm. I'll carry on with this rest and light work for a bit anyway, arthritis does often improve in summer.'

'And you're still welcome to ride Lad, as soon as that over-reach heals, 'Patsy told him. 'Just remember to concentrate a bit more.'

Then Jim, the farrier, rang Patsy and said that he had heard of a horse which might suit Mack.

'Bit of a one off, like, but be fair, you could go saying the same about Mack,' he told her. 'Gentlemen who owned it brought it over with him from Italy, kept it with a lady who takes a few liveries, and then she says he went off leaving it with her and she won't keep it for nothing. She wants someone to take it off her hands.'

'What is it like?' Patsy asked him. 'What do you mean, it's a one off?'

'Just had some unconventional riding, bit like Mack's coloured horse,' replied Jim. 'More of a thoroughbred cross type but about the right sort of size, just a bit unusual, you might say. She'd let it go for the price of the debt.'

Patsy was curious and when she told him so was Mack.

'Sounds worth a look, just to see what Jim means,' he said. 'It was you Jim told about it, can you ring the woman?'

Patsy did so and a strong no-nonsense voice told her Jim had mentioned Mack and they were welcome to take a look.

'It's no use to me,' she said. 'I've enough to ride and cobs are my type. Yours too, I think, I've seen your stallion at the shows. Don't want a swop, do you?'

Patsy assured her that she did not.

'Pity,' she was told. 'Never mind, you come and see this animal and we'll take it from there.'

The address was along the coast a few miles towards St. David's and a narrow lane led them along the top of cliffs to a solid looking house with fields dropping away towards the sea.

'Be wild up here in a gale,' said Mack, but the house was well shielded by a thicket of thorn and fir trees and the stables were in an old farmyard at the side.

The owner, 'Mrs. Lambert, call me Iris,' was a good-looking lady in her forties, well preserved with well-cut fair hair. Her designer jeans fitted tightly and she wore a thin gold chain in the neck of her blue sweater, which also fitted firmly. Patsy saw Mack's appreciative glance and trod firmly on his toe.

Iris, who had seen the look, grinned with a flash of very white teeth and offered coffee.

'Perhaps we could come to that later,' Mack told her. 'Have a look at the horse and then we'll know if there's anything to discuss.'

'Sensible,' Iris gave Mack's arm a firm pat and stepped out of the door and into a waiting pair of yard boots. 'This way.'

The farm buildings were clearly mainly given over to horses. Two attractive cob heads looked over their doors and another head appeared at a third. This was quite different, long and dished and Arab style, with a crooked white streak between challenging large eyes. Iris unhooked a head collar from a nearby hook and opened the door.

'This is Aries,' she told them. 'Nothing nasty about him but he's never been taught many manners.'

She put the head collar on and led the horse out. He was about sixteen hands, a dark but shining liver chestnut with a look of substance in spite of his clearly part Arab blood.

'Part Barb, something part thoroughbred I should think, Arab sire,' Iris told them as the horse swung round her. He had a longish back and light neck and Patsy suspected that he would ride hollow. Iris jerked the rope and the horse stood, head high and long ears pricked. He was certainly not conventional looking but there was a bold forward look about his eyes and and when Mack went to pat him he turned a swiftly enquiring head and pricked ears to nuzzle him.

'He likes men,' there was something dry about the way she said it. 'Bit misled of him from the way his owner abandoned him here but we can all make mistakes.'

'He could be a bit too much of a thoroughbred for what I want.' Mack was obviously thinking of his problems with Lad.'

'What has he done?' Patsy asked her. 'Has he been on rough ground?'

'So it seemed,' said Iris. 'Owner used to go all over the place with him. Especially keen on the beach and the dunes.'

'Can we watch you on him?' Patsy asked her, but Iris shook her head.

'Better you try him yourself,' she told them. 'If you see me it'll give the wrong impression. I seem to be good at that.'

There was definitely a double meaning here but Patsy decided not to pursue it and Mack, obviously thinking the same, said that he was willing to ride. Iris led the horse back into his stable while she fetched his tack and Patsy and Mack went in with him to feel legs and pick up feet and get some feel of the horse's character.

'I rather think someone let our Iris down,' said Mack. 'And I don't mean the horse.'

Iris came back with a light flat saddle and a bridle with a thick snaffle bit and the horse peacefully accepted having them on.

'He'd been ridden bareback quite a bit,' she told them. 'Apparently he'd been bred and started in work with the Pialo de Siena in mind. They ride them bareback in that.'

'Is that the crazy race round the town square?' Pasty asked her, and Iris said that it was.

'Taken very seriously I believe,' she said. 'Honour of the Italian areas for which each horse competes. They're a bit like our counties but much more so. Trouble is, I understand, those that don't make the final selection can get a bit lost. This one's owner had ridden him training and wanted to keep him from a rough future.'

She led the horse out and held him at the mounting block for Mack to get into the saddle.

It was clear at once that he and the horse suited each other in appearance anyway. Mack's long legs came naturally into a comfortable position and his height made a comfortable balance. Iris went ahead to open the gate into a sand school and the horse went calmly in. Patsy and Iris leaned on the gate to watch.

Aries did not look schooled, he went with his head high and back hollow but he moved straight and well and his stride was long and free. He had a light, active trot and a floating Arab canter and he was thoroughly forward going, almost too much so for the confines of the school. Mack rode him with the long rein he liked with Osbourne and left the horse to find his own balance.

'Van rode him like that, all free and forward,' Iris told Patsy. 'Let's see what they make of each other in the field.'

She opened another gate which led into an open field, sloping down towards the cliff and the sea.

There was a brisk wind blowing out here; below the

cliffs there were white crests on the waves and the gorse bushes which grew along the edge were bent inwards by what was obviously the prevailing wind. There were several rough coated ponies grazing in the spot of shelter behind them and the ground was uneven and rutted in places. Aries went through the gate without flinching from the wind or showing excitement about the ponies and Mack sent him straight into a trot with a loose rein in his usual style. Beside Patsy Iris shook her head.

'Might be Van out there,' she said. 'Same sort of riding, forward and free. Quite impressive in its way.'

'Jim said he, Van is it, went home suddenly without his horse,' Patsy was curious. 'Did he have some problem with him?'

'Not with the horse,' said Iris. 'With...other things. He came over to join his brother running an Italian bistro down in Cardigan. There was some trouble about duty free liquor and Van wanted out. One day he was here, next no sign of him. I wasn't going to fund the horse's keep when he already owed me.'

'Smuggling?' Mack would love that story, thought Patsy, he could use it in his books.

'Seemed like it. Probably thought he'd found good cover up here with the barns and the horses,' Iris was watching Mack let Aries stretch into a gallop. 'And a soft touch of a woman owner who'd keep quiet with a bit of encouragement.'

Mack was obviously enjoying his ride. His way of riding Osbourne seemed to fit Aries just as well and even over the rough patches of ground the horse was happily finding his own balance.

He checked without fighting when Mack tightened the reins and they came back towards the gate at a controllable trot.

'Nice horse,' said Mack. 'Bit different to my old boy but he seems to know what I want without too much finesse. What are you asking for him?'

'As I told Jim I just want to cover my bill and see the back of him,' Iris told him. 'I don't like being had. Five hundred and no come back, if he doesn't suit sell him on or put him in Llanybydder sale. As far as I know he's sound and he's only a seven-year-old. '

'Are you happy to have him with us?' Mack asked Patsy, and she nodded.

'You seem to get on with him so why not?' she patted the horse as Iris opened the gate. 'We can sort out a place for him, with Osbourne maybe. We can come back with the box after lunch.'

'You're welcome to have that tack with him if you want it,' Iris told them. 'Fifty more, it's no use for any of mine.'

They refused Iris's rather half-heated offer of coffee and on the way home Patsy told Mack the smuggling story and he laughed.

'I suspect there's something a bit more personal involved,' he said. 'But I have to buy the horse after that. They don't often come with the plot of a book attached.'

They collected Aries as arranged. The horse loaded calmly into the Transit and Iris accepted the money.

'Now to see what the Italian job makes of his new

home,' said Mack, as they drove back along the cliff road.

CHAPTER FOUR

Whatever his background the new horse seemed happy with his new home. Osbourne and Boy accepted him with no more than token sniffing and squealing and followed him as he set off at his long striding trot to explore. In the next field Fly came at a challenging trot to investigate but
Aries ignored him.
'Do you really think he'll cope on the hills with those long legs?' asked Katy. 'It'll be a bit of a change from racehorse training.'
'But that wasn't conventional,' Patsy pointed out.
'Like everything else about him, by the sound of it,' Katy grinned. 'Maybe he will suit you, Mack, the whole thing sounds like fiction. When are you going to ride him out?'
'Couple of days,' said Mack. 'Give him time settle in first.'
Work on the new cottage was proceeding more smoothly with Al sorting out some of the basic problems although it had meant partly dismantling the stonework holding the new bigger window which was designed to give a good view down the field to the woods.

'The measurements didn't take notice of the old stone,' he told Patsy, when she was again delivering Tomos, on Buzz, to Rhianne. 'You have to have a feel for what it likes, not try too much chipping and forcing. Stone has a mind of its own.'

It was the first thing Al had said that made Patsy see him as something different to the normal builders and gave a hint to how he and Forrest's mother thought. Up to now she had taken it that the green image was just something that he indulged in for her sake but watching him handle the stone she could see that he had more in common with Ana's thinking than she had realised. When she mentioned it to Forrest he agreed.

'It's about working with things,' he said. 'Things that grow or have ways of their own. Mum's got her bees settled in by moving their hives to where she reckons they showed they wanted them and same with the herbs and stuff she's growing. She says you just have to listen to stuff to get it right.'

He certainly seemed to have got the right touch with Nell. Now that she knew he would be coming and give her something to do she had lost her need to wander. She was happy to have him ride her and the blind eye did not seem to be a problem, but she was not as happy with a different rider. When Katy tried she was at once tense and anxious, turning her head to look and bumping into the gate because she had misjudged it.

'So much for making her into a trekking pony,' said Katy. 'And Forrest will get too big and heavy when he's a bit older. Should we try getting her in foal again, Fly would be happy to oblige if she'd have him.'

But when Patsy tried putting Nell out with her handsome stallion Nell was not interested. After kicking him firmly when he approached she returned to her usual escape by jumping the gate out of his field and demanding to be let back in with her daughter and the donkeys.

'I think that was a definite no thanks,' said Katy, as Nell marched away down her own field swishing her tail indignantly.

Mack said that he had given Aries enough time to settle. He had ridden Osbourne again and been sorry to find no improvement and he was eager to discover just what sort of horse he had bought.

Katy had gone to Carmarthen in search of something she needed for her computer and taken Tomos with her in Patsy's car.

It was a good time to ride and Patsy and Mack set out with Patsy on Golly for solid support.

'Green road and lanes today,' Suggested Patsy. 'Before you launch off into the wilds with him.'

Mack agreed that this was sensible.

The dark chestnut horse seemed quite happy. He strode out in his long, free walk and Golly had to break frequently into a jog to keep up. Round the first bend they met Ethan driving a tractor towing a trailer load of sugar beets. Aries threw up his head to stare at it but when Mack steered him into a nearby passing place he stood with Golly close behind him as it crawled past.

'Can't ask for much better than that,' said Mack, as they moved on.

The lanes were wet from an earlier shower and now with the sun out everything was shining. Aries splashed cheerfully through the puddles and they turned into the green bridleway that followed the rising land upwards between newly green banks of brambles and tangled tendrils of rose bushes towards the endless clarity of the blue sky. Golly, ready for the canter which he knew was coming, broke into a jog.
'Right, let's go,' Mack called back to her, and he loosened his reins and leant forward. Aries did not hesitate; the long stride broke straight into a canter and they were off. Clattering behind over a patch of loose stones Patsy saw the flying red tail drawing away, the stones and clumps of mud kicked back, and the horse sure footed and easy over the rough ground. As the going improved on the rising track Aries seemed almost to float in the way of his Arab ancestors and Patsy wondered if Mack had a hope of stopping as the surfaced lane ahead drew closer but there was no problem. As Mack sat down and took up a feel on the reins the horse checked and by the time Golly, who had been pulling hard himself, came alongside he was back to a trot. Mack was beaming, his face red from the wind, and as Aries slowed to a walk he leaned forward to give him an enthusiastic pat
'That was quite something,' he said. 'My old boy is great but this one is a real flyer, and he seems to have kept some sense with it. He should have no problem with the moor.'
Patsy had rarely seen him so enthusiastic. Mack

normally rode for safe, enjoyable transport through his much-loved country but this time it was the horse that he was centred on.

Riding back into the yard later Patsy turned from closing the gate to see Mack staring towards the field.

'There was someone in with Nell and her friends,' he said. 'I just saw them nipping away down the path.'

'Not Forrest?' Patsy asked him, and Mack said no.

'Smaller and long haired, female,' he told her. Nell was staring that way as well with Muff beside her.

'Stay here, 'Patsy told him. 'Come on Golly, let's catch them.'

Golly went off with a will in pursuit leaving Mack coping with the startled Aries. At the top of the slope down into the trees Patsy saw their intruder hiding behind a holly bush and Golly snorted to a stop.

'Who is it?' Patsy called. 'Come on, I don't bite, neither does Golly.'

The intruder stepped back into the path and proved to be a girl of about twelve with long brown hair and Forrest's direct brown eyes. She was dressed in tidy dark trousers and a navy sweater which looked like school wear and she looked defiant.

'I came to see Moonlight's baby,' she said, 'Forrest wouldn't tell me where she was so I got in the back of Dad's van when they thought I'd got the school bus.'

'I take it Moonlight is our Nell,' said Patsy. 'You'd better come with me, and tell someone where you are before the school rings your Mum.'

'I don't like school,' Brook told her. 'I don't mind learning but they tease me because we live differently.'

She looked defiant. Patsy, imagining the teasing, felt sympathetic. She dropped down off Golly and beckoned. 'Come on, you can ride Golly back if you like,' she said and the girl's expression changed happily.

'Oh yes please,' she said, and Patsy gave her a leg up onto Golly's broad back. It was obvious that Brooke had been on a horse before. She knew how to hold the reins and when Patsy pulled the stirrups up a couple of holes she put her feet into them quite naturally. With Patsy walking by his head Golly carried her cheerfully back to the yard.

'Forrest's sister I presume,' said Mack, when they arrived. 'Your Mother rang your Dad to see if he knew where you were when the school told her you were missing. I told him I thought you were here.'

'She won't make me go now,' said Brooke happily. 'She thinks it's her fault I get teased.'

'But you need to reassure your Dad,' Patsy told her. 'Stay there and Golly can carry you down to where he's working. Alright with you Mack?'

'Carry on, I'll get Italy back in his field and look out something for lunch.' Mack told her.

'So I was right,' said Al, when Golly came round the corner with Brooke looking happy on his back.

'Suppose you stowed away. It's a good thing Forrest guessed what you'd done or we'd have had search parties out.'

Brooke said that she was sorry and Al said, 'Alright. Let me get this stone settled then I'll have to drive you back.'

Patsy asked him how he was getting on and Al said 'Slower than I'd like. Seems one thing after another don't go easy. The boys are finding the same inside.'

Brooke had gone to look inside the cottage herself and now she came back wrinkling her nose.

'It doesn't like me,' she said. 'And it's cold. Maybe Mum should have a look.'

'How can a place not like you?' Patsy asked her, although she thought that she knew what Brooke meant. There had always been something unwelcoming about the building.

'Not really your Mum's thing,' Al told her. 'Can't be rearranging rooms that are only half built.'

Brooke did not look convinced but then Forrest appeared and said he'd finished the job with Ethan and John wanted Ethan for the sheep.

'Shame you aren't old enough to drive,' Al told him. 'Or you could drop your sister back at her school.'

'I'll take her,' offered Patsy. 'But you can walk back with me on Golly now, Brooke. I'm not doing all the work.'

'Do I have to go to school?' Brooke looked rebellious but Al said 'Yes. We'll be in trouble if you don't go, you know that.'

'I suppose,' Brooke patted Golly as Patsy mounted him. 'Can I come and see him, and Moonlight and the other horses, again?'

'So long as your mother agrees,' Patsy told her, and Brooke walked fairly cheerfully back to the yard beside Golly.

Mack was outside talking to a stranger when they

got there, a woman with long brown hair over her shoulders. She was dressed in loose cotton trousers and a well-worn green sweater and she had Patsy's usually stand-offish old cat rubbing and purring happily in her arms.

'Mum,' said Brooke, as Patsy had already guessed. 'She always finds a cat, they love her. She says it's because they know she's a witch and cats are a sort of witch themselves.'

The woman turned to greet them and Patsy saw silvery brown eyes matching silver streaks in her hair and had little difficulty in believing it might be true.

'This is Ana,' Mack told Patsy. 'Come in search of her errant daughter.'

'Not much doubt about where I'd find you,' said Ana. 'Not once Forrest talked about the horses. But it's school now. Whatever we both think about formal education it's the law of this land that you have to go.'

'And your Mum's brought you transport,' Mack sounded amused. 'Riding one here and leading one as well as if they had four legs, not two wheels.'

There were two bikes leaning on the mounting block. The woman was looking at Patsy who had the feeling that those silvery eyes could completely evaluate her.

'And you're Patsy, 'Ana smiled. 'Another seeing cat person like me. Thank you for indulging my daughter's horse affinity.'

She put the cat gently down on the block and set the bicycles on their wheels. 'Come on Brooke, before the education authorities descend on us. Thank you both, I suspect you won't have seen the last of my family.'

She tilted the smaller bike towards Brooke who unwillingly took the handlebars and her mother stepped over her own bike.

'Thank you,' said Brooke. 'I can come again can't I?'

Patsy agreed and with Ana urging her on Brooke bounced over the cattle grid and the two of them vanished up the lane. Mack was grinning as Patsy turned to lead Golly into the stable.

'Quite a family,' he said. 'How does a steady fellow like Al cope with them?'

'He may be steady but he isn't quite so prosaic as he seems,' Patsy remembered Al's feeling for stone. 'But I suspect he does keep a balance.'

The next holiday booking in the completed cottage was the one by the horse owning people. Gareth and Ethan had built a solid post and rail fence to make a safe separate turn out for them and Patsy had cleared stored bales of wood chips and mucking out tools out of her two spare stables.

The visitors arrived with the horses in a trailer behind a smart Land Rover and the driver, a cheerful looking lady with short blond hair, introduced herself as Myra Robson and her daughter as Verity. Verity had long blond hair and an irritable expression and she looked impatient as her mother chatted to Patsy and exclaimed about the beautiful scenery and the resident animals.

'Of course we saw the little white one in that famous video,' she said. 'Such a sweetie, and who is that? He's magnificent.' This as Fly shouted his usual challenging shriek as he heard strange horses in the trailer.

'My Welsh Cob, Heddfa Aur,' Patsy was proud of her horse. 'Golden Flight. He's been cob champion at the Royal Welsh.'

Myra was starting towards the fence for a closer look but Verity said 'Oh, come on Mother. You can see the local champions later. I want to get Challenger out.'

'Alright, later,' Myra turned back to the trailer and the front ramp came down to show a well-bred bay head. The horse did not look particularly excited by the prospect of new surroundings and when untied he came composedly down the ramp. He was about sixteen hands, a well-made part thoroughbred wrapped in an expensive travelling rug and travel boots. Something about him looked as though he should be full of vitality but instead he looked bored. Inside the trailer his companion whinnied and Myra went to unload a pretty grey pony of about fourteen two. He seemed a lot more interested in his new surroundings and Myra patted him.

'This is my boy, Samphire,' she said. 'He's not a champion except to me, but we have a lot of fun together.'

Verity raised despairing eyebrows and Patsy hid a smile. She had a feeling that she was going to like Myra.

Once in the stable the pony began busily to explore but the bay hung his head over the door and looked bored. 'Challenger is used to strange stables,' Myra was watching her daughter remove the horse's travel boots. 'Verity is very keen on show jumping, amateur level I suppose, but two or even more shows a week… well, except for a break during part of the lockdown which I must say I found a relief. That didn't stop it entirely, but her horse had a lot of the time stabled. He's due for a change.'

'You only think that because he's been putting in a few stops,' Verity told her. 'I still think he'd have been better going to Jed Parker's clinic for a week.'

'And I say he needs a change,' this was obviously an ongoing disagreement. 'Long hacks in open country and I believe you can manage a beach ride can't you Mrs. Mackintosh?'

'Patsy,' Patsy told her. 'Yes, there are great beach rides, either by box or a half day's hack.'

Myra said that would be great but Verity sighed resignedly.

The two horses were changed from travel to fly rugs and Challenger was equipped with protective turn out boots and Patsy led the way to the field.

It was a sheltered three acres with woods on one side and a view across the ravine behind Patsy's land to the rising sheep fields beyond. Samphire was off at a lively trot to explore and for a moment the other horse stood by the gate. Then a gust of wind rustled through the new leaves bringing a sweet breath of the open moors and the horse raised his head and pricked his ears and his eyes were suddenly bright. The grey pony was digging in the soft ground and turning round, preparing to roll, and with a sudden squeal and a kick the horse was off to join him. They went down in turn, rolling and squirming, getting up to shake and change places and rolling again. Then they were up and off, flying round the field, the bay kicking and bucking behind his friend, and Myra was laughing as her daughter exclaimed.

'A dose of freedom,' she said. 'No single strip turnout between hours of stable. I tell you Verity, this is what your horse needs.'

'Unless he ruins his legs,' Verity was unimpressed. 'And I don't see why this tearing about loose will help his jumping, it'll just him want his own way.'

'We'll see,' Myra turned away from the gate as the horses began to snatch eagerly at the grass. 'Now, we'd better un-hitch the trailer and drive round to find our own stable.'

'What will you do with them first?' Mack asked later when they were doing the evening animal rounds. The visitors were staying turned out, 'making the most of their break,' Myra had said.

'A quiet hack down to the green to let them get the feel of the moor,' said Patsy. 'Myra's keen about it but I hope that bay show jumper doesn't manage to hurt its self or there will be an awful lot of "I told you so" from her daughter.'

The two visiting horses survived the night without harming themselves and Myra and Verity brought them in to get ready to ride as agreed. Katy was working and Patsy said that just Golly out as escort was probably the safest option.

'Your new purchase is hardly a calming influence,' she told Mack, who had to agree.

There was still plenty of water everywhere on the

moor although today the sky was blue with scudding white clouds above a pair of circling buzzards. Both the visiting horses went past Patsy as she held open the gate and stopped with high heads and pricking ears to stare at this strange country. Patsy remembered Golly's amazement at the sight when she first brought him out here, his confusion about the white sheep which moved and white rocks which did not and at the lack of enclosed tracks or limits to the distances.

'Breath taking,' was Myra's comment, and Verity said, 'Is the ground really right for a performance horse like mine?'

'So long as you know which bits are real bog and go a bit steady,' Patsy told her. 'Just follow Golly,' but Verity looked unconvinced.

At the moment, after his first surprised look round, both she and her performance horse looked unimpressed by the view although the pony was staring around eagerly as Patsy led the way down towards the green with its three cottages and the farm which partly enclosed it. There was the fast-running stream to cross first on the narrow plank bridge with its single handrail. In summer the water level dropped so that it was simple to ford it but today the water was running fast and well up the banks. Myra was smiling but Verity looked less happy.

'Now this is proper riding,' said Myra. 'No school rails or coloured jumps, just space and natural obstacles.'

'If we all wanted to be cowboys,' Verity was eyeing the plank bridge doubtfully. 'Do we really have to ride across that?'

'Follow Golly,' Patsy told her. 'New horses soon get used to it when they see he doesn't care.'

Golly led the way in his usual confident fashion and Samphire scuttled across behind him looking astonished. Challenger was dithering at the edge until Verity, starting to get cross, dug her heels in at which the bay horse brought his hocks under him and leaped, clearing the whole bridge and almost knocking his grey friend over as he landed. Verity stayed with him and Myra said, 'That's one way of doing it I suppose.'

The experience had woken the horse up. He came alongside Golly with pricked ears, snorting at his own bravery, as Patsy led the way on along the twisty path between hedged fields to the green, an area of sheep and pony grazed grass between more of the few thorny hedges to be found out there.

There was a small group of wild ponies grazing there among some sheep and the visitors eyed them with amazement, Samphire all pricking ears and bright eyes, Challenger with doubt. Loose horses to him remained in fields, not out in the open. These were mares, heavy in foal, and apart from a quick glance they were not interested in the ridden horses.

'We'd better just trot,' Patsy told her companions. 'We don't want to upset them, they'll be foaling pretty soon.'

'Do they just stay out here?' asked Verity. 'They aren't really wild are they? I mean, doesn't someone own them?'

'Oh yes,' Patsy told her. 'Local farmers have grazing rights but these ponies are tough, when they're due to foal they'll know a quiet sheltered spot and just get on with it. The stallion won't be far away, he'll keep an eye on them.'

'Samphire is part Welsh,' said Myra. 'No wonder he feels happy out here, it must be bred in him.'

'Challenger is warm blood,' said Verity. 'I think his ancestors were a lot more civilised.'

That certainly seemed likely when they were past the ponies and Patsy decided it was safe to try a canter. Samphire scuttled cheerfully after Golly while Challenger, who had been looking switched off again, suddenly woke up, gave a large buck, and just avoided falling over a gorse clump by jumping over it. Verity hung on and pulled her horse's head up as they turned round the green back to the made-up lane beside it.

'At least he's woken up,' said Myra, as they slowed to a walk to step down from the grass onto the hard surface, but Verity muttered that she didn't see why making him mess about would help his jumping.

They cantered again up the long green slope between the gorse bushes to the gate. To their left the hills rose up against the breezy sky and as they reached the gate Myra was gazing up at them.

'That's where I want to go,' she said. 'Up towards the old rocks and the view.'

'We can do that tomorrow,' Patsy promised, but Verity looked doubtful.

'I thought the idea was to freshen mine up, not break his leg,' she said, but Patsy., mentally crossing her fingers, assured her that it was safe.

'I ride my ex-racehorse up there and he's fine,' she told Verity.

Back at Bryn Uchaf Mack was guarding Tomos and explained that there seemed to have been another cottage disaster.

'Ethan damaged his wrist,' he told Patsy. 'He fell off a ladder helping Al to fix some loose guttering. Rhianne's taken him to A and E and Katy's in the middle of a Zoom meeting so I took over babysitting.'

'How did he manage to fall?' Patsy asked. Ethan was used to heights and ladders from all the farm work, but Mack shrugged his shoulders.

'Al doesn't understand it,' he said. 'He was up there himself, fixing the other end, and Ethan's ladder suddenly began to go. No wind and it was on firm ground.'

Patsy felt a prickle at the back of her neck. Surely a building couldn't really have any influence, but it was odd. Mack was watching her.

'Yes,' he said. '"More things in heaven and earth" as I seem to remember saying before about something else, but it's most likely to have been a slippery bit of loose ground.'

Myra and Verity had their horses ready to turn out and Patsy agreed to go out with them again next day. Tomos was clamouring for a ride on Buzz and Patsy said that she would take him down to the farm and see if there was any news of Ethan. Mack said that he would take Osbourne for a short ride and Patsy knew that he wanted some mind clearing time before

GILLIAN BAXTER

returning to write.

CHAPTER FIVE

At the farm Al was up a ladder again with Forrest at the bottom to make sure it stayed secure. John came round from the sheep while she was there and reported that Rhianne had called to say that Ethan had broken his wrist and they were waiting for him to have it strapped up. He eyed the building balefully and said that it was a shame no-one had taken his advice about converting the corner of the main yard instead.
'Too late now,' he said. 'But maybe that's the last of it. Could be nice enough if it settles for it.'
'If what settles?' Patsy asked him, but John looked vague.
'Oh, just the luck with it,' he said, and then he turned to pay attention to Tomos, who wanted to get off Buzz to play with his collie friend and Patsy knew that he would not say any more.
Al climbed down his ladder and said he had done as much as he could until a delivery arrived with some special mortar that was on order and Forrest took Buzz to graze while Tomos and the
dog played a special game of their making which involved going round and round some piles of stones and Patsy seized the chance to go quietly into the

cottage on her own.

It was very quiet in there. Outside it was still breezy and there was a sound of restless sheep from the pens but inside the old stone walls there was silence and a feeling of chill. Patsy went through the main room into the first of the intended bedrooms and as she paused in there the door swung softly closed behind her.

'There must be a draught,' thought Patsy, but suddenly the air felt thick and the lack of light from the half-finished window made her feel stifled. Turning to the door for a moment she was afraid that it would not open but when she touched the latch it came quietly open again and she went back through the main room to the kitchen, a normal enough site of half installed units and cans of paint.

"Imagination," Patsy told herself firmly, but she could not help a feeling of relief when the easily opened back door let her back into the open air and the sight of Tomos and the dog hugging each other on the grass.

Forrest was holding Buzz. a short distance away, the donkey was grazing but it seemed to Patsy that he was keeping an ear and an eye on the cottage and as she came out his head went up and he stared at her.

'It's alright boy, just me,' Patsy told him, and Forrest patted him.

'He always keeps an eye on what's going on round there,' he said. 'It is a funny old place, when I'm helping Ethan in there we've both thought something didn't like us.'

'I suppose it's just been unused for so long,' said Patsy,

but she knew that she was not convinced.

Forrest lifted Tomos back onto the donkey and offered to lead him back and visit Nell while Al waited for his delivery. Patsy let them go ahead while she paused to speak to the group of horses in their field on the way. There was no feeling of anything here close to old Mary's cottage except deep peace and Patsy thought that however fanciful it might seem buildings, even abandoned ones, did retain something of their past inhabitants.

Back at Bryn Uchaf Mack had returned from his ride and was looking rather dejected as he brushed Osbourne down.

'I don't think rest is helping at all,' he said. 'He's keen to go out but he definitely doesn't feel right down hills. He's getting bored with the field though, waiting at the gate for attention. Maybe I should try the vet's remedy.'

'My Mum's good at helping stiff joints,' Forrest had heard him. 'People come to her for her herb stuff. I'll tell her about your old horse.'

'Worth a try,' Mack patted Osbourne. 'I really don't think he'd be happy retired.'

Patsy knew that he was right. Osbourne had always seemed to enjoy roving the hills as much as his owner did and remembering Forrest's mother Patsy found it quite possible to believe that a remedy from her might help.

Myra and Verity were in good time next morning, Myra eager to get out but Verity doubtfully eyeing the low cloud which was hanging on the hills.

'If you want to go up there to see the views I shouldn't think there'll be any,' she told her mother but Patsy, used to Preseli weather, told her to wait.

'It'll probably lift,' she said. 'And if it doesn't we might see the Preseli fairies.'

'Fairies?' Verity sounded incredulous but Patsy said, 'People surrounded by the mist suddenly find themselves touched by magic,' and Myra laughed.

'Great,' she said, 'let's go up there and see,' and Verity raised scornful eyebrows but put on her hat and fetched Challenger out of the stable.

The mist was still above them as they started along the causeway across the boggy land towards the abandoned farm and the Hafod fields but soon tendrils began to dampen the horses' manes and touch the riders faces. Verity shivered and her horse shied at a sheep which appeared suddenly out of it.

'We can canter on,' Patsy told them. 'Just stay behind Golly, the going is fine along here.'

Verity looked disbelieving but she shortened her reins and Patsy let Golly go on. Challenger came easily after him and Samphire came eagerly behind. Ahead the mist was quite thick and Patsy hoped that her confident assurance about the going would not be proved wrong by an unexpected patch of loosened stones or a dead sheep. The sound of hooves was muffled by the damp air and the view of Bedd Arthur's stones higher up was completely hidden. Then Patsy saw the clump of gorse bushes which marked the end of the Hafod fields looming out of the mist and she called, 'Trotting now, 'The other two horses came alongside as they slowed and for a few strides they seemed to be suspended in white nothingness. Then, ahead Patsy glimpsed light and suddenly the mist seemed to draw back and they broke into dazzling sunlight. The white walls enclosed them, close by everything sparkled, each twig of gorse and stem of cobweb-hung heather held the drops of mist and caught the light, and a stirring of the air sent them quivering and alive. Patsy had heard stories of the Preseli fairy lands and she had seen some beautiful and strange things up here but nothing to beat the fragile beauty of this moment.

Behind her she heard Myra exclaim and Verity draw a surprised breath. Clouds of steam from the horses were rising around them and for a moment no-one spoke. Then Myra said, 'It's really true, only fairies could live here,' and although Verity made a scornful sound Patsy knew that it was half hearted. Then, as the horses moved on along the path round round the top of the bracken covered slope, they felt the cold touch of the mist again as the sunlight was hidden and they were back in the low cloud.

'I'm so glad we saw that,' said Myra sincerely. 'I shan't forget our glimpse of magic.'

Patsy agreed with her. Mack would be sorry to have missed it, she knew, it was an experience that could build legends.

Back home, with the horses turned out, Myra was keen to make plans for next day.

'Beach ride next,' Patsy promised. 'To get the best of it we need low tide at the right time and it should be right in the late morning tomorrow.'

It wasn't only the visitors who were keen to go on a beach ride. Katy wanted to bring Boy and Mack said that he would bring Aries. Compared to the hills riding on the open beach sounded quite civilised and Patsy decided that Golly could do with a day off and she would ride Lad. It was possible to hack to the beach but it involved quite a lot of road work and Patsy proposed that they boxed the horses down. By moving the partitions she could just fit three in her lorry for a short trip and Myra was happy to bring her trailer.

It was good weather for a ride on the beach, the sky was blue with only patchy puffs of white cloud and as they drove down the steep road across Newport golf course they could see the waves rolling in with only a few flecks of foam on the breaking surf. The horses were immediately alert when they were led out, even Challenger's faintly bored expression changed as instead of the show ground he expected he saw the sandy space of the larger of the two car parks and heard the murmur of the sea. Lad had been to the beach before and so, according to 'call me Iris,' had Aries. Myra said she had taken Samphire once to a beach in Kent and he had loved it.

When everyone was mounted Patsy led the way down the ramp to the beach. The tide was well out and the firm wet sand was patched with little pools and fronds of seaweed. Lad was eager to go, remembering accompanying his previous owners string of racehorses to their gallops on the beach. Boy's eyes were wide with amazement and Challenger's head

was high and his eyes bright. Aries was calm and had obviously seen a beach before and little Samphire was bouncing with excitement. It was too early in the year for many people to be out. There were a number of dog walkers and a man fishing with a fixed line but otherwise the way was clear.
'Let's trot first,' Patsy suggested. 'Let them settle before we go any faster.'
She led the way along the open sand to where the creek cut through the sand dunes with Newport village perched on the opposite bank with its castle rising on the hill behind it. Aries came up beside her moving with his long floating stride and glancing back Patsy saw Boy cantering sideways, Challenger wide awake and very much on the bit and Samphire gathered up and eager. They passed the fisherman, keeping well behind him and his line, and then the creek was in front of them and Patsy brought Lad back to a walk and turned to lead them beside it to the edge of the surf. All the horses were keen now, used to the feel of the firm sand and ready to go. They lined up where the incoming tide met the water of the creek and the horses stared out to sea, heads high and ears pricked as they stared out over the white edging to the endless glitter of the open water.
'Beautiful,' Myra sounded awed. 'How can my husband prefer a golfing tour to this?'
'Is that where he is?' Patsy had not liked to inquire about other halves before, and Myra grinned.
'Yes, in France,' she said. 'I'm used to being a golf widow. He's a great old boy but his golf is like my

horse, his escape valve. You're lucky having someone who shares yours.'

'Yes,' Patsy looked fondly at Mack, sitting easily on Aries who was pawing the water up into a shower over his legs. 'Yes, I know I am.'

'Come on Mum, Boy wants to get moving,' Katy was restraining the excited little skewbald who was swinging in circles, and Patsy glanced along the shoreline. The fisherman had reeled in his line and the way was clear.

'Right,' she said. 'Let's see what they're all made of.'

She turned Lad along the edge of the sand where the last ripples of surf were lapping and loosened the reins. Lad had no doubt what that meant, he took hold of the bit and they were away, sand and water flying and Aries taking the lead with Samphire close behind. Patsy leaned forward and let him go, seeing Challenger's nose alongside and hearing Katy telling Boy to steady just behind. Spray from the galloping feet flew into her face and startled seagulls rose from the beach ahead. People walking dogs paused to watch and some boys playing on the edge of the dunes turned round. Then the end of the beach with its rocks and the cliff rising behind it were coming close and in front Mack was

sitting up and tightening slack reins. They finished in an untidy group, steaming excited horses and even Verity laughing from the thrill of it.

'Great,' said Myra. 'I vote we trot back and do it again.'

Everyone agreed and next time it turned into a genuine race with Lad, Aries, and even Challenger vying for the lead.

It was Aries who reached the rocks first, again coming sensibly back to a trot when Mack asked him, and Patsy had a struggle to stop Lad in time to avoid scrambling through the first rock pool. Verity pulled Challenger aside to where softening sand checked him and Boy and Samphire turned the other way into the water.

'He doesn't look stale now,' Myra told her daughter as Verity brought a very bright-eyed Challenger back to the group, but Verity refused to be impressed.

'I still don't see that it'll help his jumping.' she said.

'Wait and see. He's enjoying himself anyway,' Myra told her.

'Let's wade them,' Patsy turned Lad into the water and the others followed. All the horses were happy to wade, splashing along, pawing up great waves of the sparkling salt water over their legs, and Boy suddenly decided that he wanted to roll in it.

'Watch out,' Patsy was just in time as Boy's legs began to fold and Katy hastily dug in her heels.

They walked the horses back along the edge of the water, splashing through the surf, and beside Patsy Mack smiled, patting his horse's wet dark red neck.

'I think he's done this before,' he said, and a few strides further on this was confirmed when two of the boys who had been digging in the edge of the dunes ran across to them.

'Hey, Mister,' they splashed into the water close to Aries. 'In't that Van's horse?'

'I think that's right,' Mack told him. 'Do you know

him?'

'He used to come down here with that horse, swimming with it,' the boy informed them. 'No saddle, he didn't have, just rode without. He used to go right far out, the old horse can't half swim. Are you going swimming?'

'Not with a saddle,' said Mack. 'But it's quite an idea.'

'Not today, it isn't,' Patsy had visions of Rhianne's two visitors being swept out to sea. She knew that Mack was quite capable of taking Aries's saddle off and trying it.

'What else did Van do with him?' Mack asked. The two boys were keeping pace with them as the horses walked along the surf and the boy grinned.

'He'd give us a great show,' he said. 'Running him up and down the dunes, no slowing down, jumping the gaps, like a circus it was. Are you his friend or something?'

Something like that,' Mack told him. 'He had to go away.'

'Never have thought he'd leave the old horse,' the boy sounded disillusioned. He reached up to pat Aries and the horse dipped his nose to him.

'I wonder if we quite got the true story from Iris,' said Mack thoughtfully as they rode on. 'She seemed pretty bitter about him but he seems to have impressed that lad.'

Patsy thought that he might be right. Iris's version of events could have been rather one sided.

Back home the horses were relaxed and ready to go out and roll. Osbourne was at his gate and Mack made a fuss of him after he had led Aries loose.

'He thinks he's missed out on something,' he told Patsy. 'He loves the beach, I reckon he knows where we've been, Aries must smell of it.'

Patsy thought it was quite likely and she came to give Osbourne a carrot.

'Why don't you try the Bute?' she asked Mack. 'He will get bored just turned out, he's never been used to it. If it doesn't agree with him you don't have to go on. Will you want to ride him so much anyway now you've got the new one?'

'Italy's great but it isn't the same,' Mack let the old horse rub on him. 'Sounds sentimental but this fellow and me just connect. Bit like old shoes fit best I suppose.'

Patsy knew what he meant. Osbourne and Mack had been partners for a long time.

'Give the stuff a try,' she told him, and Mack said thoughtfully 'or I could take up Forrest's suggestion about Ana's herbs. I'll give it a bit longer.'

CHAPTER SIX

Myra said that she and Verity would give their horses the next day off.
'The weather forecast looks good,' she said. 'We thought we'd take the chance for a day out to
go on a boat trip to Skomer to see the puffins.'
It was one of Pembrokeshire's famous attractions, the boat trip across from the mainland to the wild little island with its nesting puffins and Manx Shearwaters and its steep cliffs with the thousands of other nesting sea birds. Patsy wished them a good trip. It would do their horses good to have a day off and she had a mare booked in to be covered by Fly.
Ethan was frustrated by his wrist. He lived in a caravan at the side of the farmhouse and he liked to be active, working on the farm and more recently on the cottage and he was bored with the restrictions of the injury. He spent a part of the spare time with his phone and one of the people he exchanged texts with was Summer.
'She passed her driving test first go,' he told Patsy. 'I bet I that Dad of hers buys her a car next. '
'She must be pleased about that,' said Patsy, and Ethan said that she was. 'But she'd still be more pleased if

he'd keep that promise about the horse. She says she reckons it's really Tabitha that doesn't want that.'

Patsy could well believe it. Horses had never found much favour with Mack's ex-wife with whom Summer, as her stepdaughter, had a prickly relationship. No doubt Tabitha would be looking forward to her going away to university, taking away the responsibility and leaving her with Flynn's undivided attention.

Katy seized the chance next morning to bring her young grey horse in and make a start on his training. Smokey was bred to compete one day as an eventer and dressage horse and he was starting to look the part, still growing, which showed in his high hind quarters, but well-made and with the promise to be athletic. He had been lunged before and he was going well, trotting and cantering on either rein, and he had worn a saddle and bridle. Katy lunged him in these and then she brought him to a halt and said, 'He's really sensible. What about backing him?'

It seemed a good moment and Patsy agreed.

In the stable Katy used a grooming box as a block and stood on it to rest her weight across her horse's back and Smokey turned his head to nuzzle her. He seemed to understand what she was doing and when Katy, with Patsy at his head, swung her leg slowly across to sit on him he hardly stiffened.

Patsy led him round the stable and Katy patted and praised him before carefully dismounting.

'He felt terrific,' she said. 'There was plenty in front of me and he's a comfortable width. I wish I could start riding him properly.'

'He's only three,' Patsy reminded her as she started to unsaddle the young horse. 'If you put too much strain on him you could start all kind of future soundness problems.'

'I suppose so,' Katy was only half convinced. 'But some horses get ridden at three.'

'And a good few end up with bad backs or leg problems,' Patsy told her, although Katy still looked unconvinced. Patsy suspected that watching Mack with his spectacular new horse had made her envious. Aries seemed to be in danger of stirring the peaceful balance among the riding partnerships.

Fly's mare arrived, a Welsh cob with showy good looks to match his. They normally did the covering the most natural way, letting the mare run loose with the stallion as soon as they got to know each other. Patsy went through the usual routine of putting her in what she called 'the courting strip alongside his field and Heddfa Aur changed from being a fairly amenable riding horse to a fiery pack of golden masculine energy as he pranced along the fence line. The mare was obviously impressed and Patsy knew that she could very soon put them together.

Myra and Verity reported a great day out on Skomer but they were were keen to ride again and Patsy decided to take them to the woods at Ty Canol nature reserve. Katy had to work and Mack said that he would take Osbourne for a slow meander on the moor.

It was beautiful in the woods. The trees were tall, smooth trunks reaching up to the canopy of bright young leaves, and the tracks were soft with many years of fallen leaves. Deep ditches of clear water ran under and beside them and in places these were crossed by rather slippery wooden bridges. Golly and Samphire picked their way gingerly over them but Challenger preferred to jump, clearing them with every appearance of enjoying it. Myra said, 'Not much doubt about his jumping here,' but Verity said that it was rather different to show jumping.

'Which is just what he needs, 'Myra told her but she refused to be convinced.

Where the trees opened out to shady clearings the bluebells were in flower, drifts of them in a blue mist, their scent sweet and heavy in the warming air.

'Glorious,' Myra was taking deep breaths of the scent and even Verity looked blissful. The smell of the damp spring earth mingled with that of the flowers and the horses' hooves disturbed the questing bees, taking their fill of the nectar after the winter bleakness.

They cantered on up a green track after the glade and as they headed out towards the back road for home Myra exclaimed at the sight of Pentre Ifan, the Neolithic burial chamber, its huge capstone dominating the skyline as it had done for thousands of years.

'I've always wanted to visit it,' she told Patsy. 'Verity and I went up the first evening we were here.

Such a feeling of stillness, it makes sense of eternity,'

'Yes,' Patsy knew what she meant. 'Time doesn't seem to mean the same when you step under that stone. It must be what its builders meant, placing their ancestors in such a place.'

'Claustrophobic,' said Verity. 'Imagine it covered in turf with you inside. '

Then Samphire shied as a squirrel dashed across the lane and Myra laughed.

'Trust you to think of something like that,' she said. 'There certainly isn't anything else claustrophobic round here.'

Then the hedges hid the stones from sight and they pulled into the side to let a tractor rattle past. It was time to trot on before the lane led them downhill towards the track for home.

Mack was not happy about Osbourne.

'He really felt uncomfortable on the hill,' he told Patsy. 'I think I will give that Bute a try. He won't be happy just vegetating in the field like the ponies do.'

There proved to be one snag to his decision. Osbourne flatly refused to eat the stuff even disguised in his feed with a spoonful of brown sugar.

'Try it in an apple,' suggested Patsy and Mack did so, cutting out the core and putting the powder into the hole. Osbourne took a bite and proceeded to spit it all out, snorting and shaking his head so bits stuck to Mack's sweater and in his hair. He then turned his back on them and put his head in the corner, looking deeply offended.

'You'll have to mix it with a bit of water and try syringing it into his mouth,' said Patsy, and Mack said he would try that way next day.

'He must have got a bit now,' he said. 'I don't want to start a real problem with him. I think it's time to have a word with Forrest's mother. I'll get Forrest to ask her to have a look.'

Ana came round the next day, peddling in on her bicycle and handing Patsy a jar of glistening clear honey from her bees.

'They found a great crop of clover last year,' she said. 'You'll be able to taste it. Now, can I have a word with your horse.'

Osbourne was at the gate, ears pricked with interest at the visitor, and Mack left his gardening to fetch him in. Ana stroked his face thoughtfully. Osbourne lowered his head to her, pressing his face against her waist and seeming to communicate. After a couple of minutes Ana nodded.

'I think I've got it,' she said. 'Walk him down the yard and I'll make sure.'

Mack did so and as the horse turned the stiffness in his hocks showed up. Mack led him back and again Osbourne reached his head out for Ana's hands.

'A bit of wear, haven't you boy,' she said to him. 'I can make something up that'll help. Forrest can bring it over.'

She was very convincing but Patsy remained slightly sceptical. It took no special knowledge to guess at arthritis in an aged horse.

'Any risk it might have any side effects?' she asked, and Ana smiled.

'It's got some well-tried ingredients,' she said. 'Some vets have been known to use them although they aren't conventional. I'm a registered herbalist though and I can promise they'll do him no harm or make him feel dopey.'

Mack thanked her and Ana said, 'Now, Forrest told me you'd got a cottage with an unhappy feel about it. House clearing is something else I do, although usually occupied ones. I could have a look if you like.'

Mack was stroking Osbourne's neck, not catching Patsy's eye, and she knew that he was leaving this to her. She was dithering, imagining John's probable reaction, but then her old cat emerged from one of her cosy daytime sleeping spots and ran straight to Ana with her tail up in greeting and reached up in a very unusual request to be picked up. There obviously was something special about Ana and Patsy made up her mind.

'Yes,' she said. 'I'd really like to know what you thought. There is something there that doesn't feel quite right.'

Osbourne looked peacefully sleepy and the cat, now in Ana's arms, completed the impression that here was someone they could trust. Patsy glanced towards Mack and he nodded. Patsy knew that he agreed.

Work on the cottage had been held up while Al waited for his delivery and it was very quiet. Ethan was in his caravan and Forrest had taken Nell for a long reining session in the wood. Ana said that she would go in alone and get a feel of it and Patsy sat on a sawhorse to wait. The stillness felt almost un-natural. There were swallows swooping in and out of the farm buildings nearby and

a pair of Jackdaws discussing a nest in one of the chimneys of Rhianne's house but there were no birds close to the cottage. John and Rhianne were not there, having gone shopping in Haverfordwest, and Patsy wondered if she should have consulted them before agreeing to Ana's visit. She was starting to feel uneasy when Ana emerged and the door banged shut behind her.

'Resentment,' she said. 'That's what I felt in there. Something resented me being there. Has someone who lived there been unfairly blamed for something?'

'Not so far as I know,' Patsy told her. 'Although there was a serious accident here once.

Someone had a fall and someone was blamed for it, but it wasn't anyone actually living here.'

'Perhaps they blamed the house,' said Ana, and Patsy, remembering Rhianne's story, realised that she was right. When she told Ana about Eirig's fall Ana nodded.

'That could be part of it,' she sad. 'Buildings hold memories, and this one resents the one it has, although there might be something else as well. I can try some herbal remedies, camomile...lemon balm, rose...I'll work out a mixture. And it needs forgiveness...perhaps even an apology.'

It sounded crazy but, looking at the blank, closed look of the building Patsy found that she could believe it. Ana was still thinking and now she said 'Bay trees outside the door, they bring positive energy. I see there's an old rosemary bush at the back already, I wonder what that was for, remembrance, or just for cooking.   Perhaps some welcoming flowers inside, roses, and gladiolus, and something happy...photos, a

cherished bit of china, anything.'
Patsy nodded and thanked her but she could not help still feeling sceptical. Could there really be anything in such ideas?
Back at Bryn Uchaf Ana paused to watch Osbourne, back in his field, and Mack thanked her for looking at him.
'Try my paste,' she told him. 'I promise it'll do him no harm, and at least it tastes better than the vet's stuff. Once you've put it on his tongue he'll be asking for more.'
She peddled off and Mack, watching her go, said 'A very impressive practitioner. I can almost believe in her.'
'She certainly felt something in that cottage,' Patsy told him what Ana had said. 'But I think it could take a bit more than herbs to sort it out.'
As they had been expecting now that Eleri had finished her temporary return to nursing she was coming to collect her ponies. They had been at Bryn Uchaf since the start of the Covid crisis and she said how much she had missed them. Her mare, West Wind, knew her at once, coming up her field at a trot, her pretty daughter, Summer Breeze, coming along behind. She was noticeably Fly's offspring with his golden colouring and flaxen mane and tail, and as a four-year-old she looked mature and ready for the next stage in her life. Eleri, who had visibly lost weight and looked older, hugged her mare and Patsy could see that she was almost in tears.
'Sometimes I thought this would never happen, I'd be

stuck in that frantic world for ever,' she said. 'In the worst of it, when we didn't understand the virus at all, it just seemed overwhelming but we finally got to grips with it and here we are, almost back to normal.'

Breeze came nosing for attention and Eleri hugged her as well.

'Time she was broken in,' she said. 'I've dreamed of it. I can't wait to get started. Thank you so much for taking such good care of them.'

'Thank you for letting Katy ride West,' Patsy told her. 'She really enjoyed it.'

'And I enjoyed the videos of her dancing to that choreographer man's great music,' said Eleri. 'I used to watch it on my pad when I was too tired to sleep.'

'If you want any help with Breeze just let me know,' Patsy told her and Eleri said that she would. They loaded the ponies into her trailer and Katy came out to thank Eleri herself. She and Patsy watched her drive out and Katy sighed.

'I'll miss that little cob,' she said. 'Time to go on with backing my own competition horse. Now Fly's back on stud duties I'm going to be short of something to ride.'

'You've got Boy,' Patsy reminded her. 'And you can ride Lad.'

'So long as Golly stands up to all this escorting,' said Katy. 'Why was I stupid enough to let Goldie get herself caught by that colt on the hill.'

The only reply to that would be 'I did warn you', from Patsy which would not be well received. She decided to keep quiet.

Ana came back next day with a jar of her paste for

Osbourne.

'Put a tablespoon full of this on the back of his tongue with a spatula,' she told Mack. 'Once he's tasted it he won't object. And these,' she handed Patsy a canvas bag, 'are for the cottage. Put a bowl of them in each room and try the flowers as well. I don't think it will clear easily. There's a very strong emotion caught up in there.'

She stroked the attentive cat and smiled at the sight of Muff playing in the field with Buzz.

'Now there is a happy emotion,' she said. 'It surrounds that little creature. No one seeing her could miss some sense of it.'

'That's what was said about the video of her,' Patsy told her. 'That it made people feel happy.'

Ana nodded and collected her bicycle.

'Forrest can tell me how the horse gets on,' she said. 'But I think you'll find it helps. And good luck with the cottage.'

She peddled off and Mack opened the jar, sniffed the contents, and smiled.

'It certainly smells pretty appetising,' he said. 'Something about it reminds me of my student days. I wonder if it's legal. Let's see what the old boy thinks.'

Osbourne was suspicious at first, putting his nose in the air and clenching his teeth, and when Mack got a scrap on his tongue he raised his upper lip, smelling and testing, and then his ears pricked and he reached out his nose to the wooden scapula. Mack grinned.

'That's one clever lady,' he said. 'I wonder who else she supplies with arthritis remedies. Here you go then mate, have the rest.'

Osbourne was obviously delighted and Mack patted him.

'Now we wait to see if it does the job,' he told Patsy.

With a feeling that it should be done without waiting for onlookers or comment Patsy took the herbs down to the cottage after work on it had stopped for the day. Rhianne came in with her, bringing some attractive blue and gold bowls from a set of her own. There was the now familiar feeling of a lack of welcome when they shut the door and Rhianne shivered slightly.

'John was right,' she said. 'The edge of the yard would have been a better choice, although this should have been more attractive, with the view over the fields for the visitors, look, but too late now.'

They filled the bowls with the sweet-smelling herbs and set them out. The atmosphere of the cottage did not change and when Rhianne turned to close the door as they left a sudden breeze slammed it shut and caught her finger. Sucking it she glared back at the door.

'Alright, fair play, we're going now,' she told the cottage, and she and Patsy looked at each other.

'Did I really say that?' she asked, and they both shivered slightly.

Osbourne looked sound next morning.

'His joints even feel cooler,' Mack told Patsy, who went to feel them herself. 'Ana seems to know what she's doing whatever her secret is. Where are you taking the visitors this morning?'

'They're taking a day out,' said Patsy. 'Having a trip to

St. David's to look at the cathedral. We could ride if you want, try the treatment out, I'll bring Lad, Golly needs a day off.'

Out on the hill Osbourne seemed his old self, cantering happily along beside Lad and descending the steep path down with no sign of discomfort.

'Long may it last,' said Mack. 'Aries is great fun but it's not the same. You can't drift off when you're riding him.'

'Room for both,' Patsy told him. 'It won't do Osbourne any harm to slow up a bit if his joints are getting a bit worn.'

They were all getting a bit of wear like the horses, she knew, there were times when her own joints got a bit sore, but cantering towards home on her eager little racehorse and seeing Mack looking as supple as ever on the big skewbald she felt that, hopefully, they all still had plenty of active life ahead.

The result of Goldie's adventure was due very soon and the mare looked well. This would be her third foal, Heddfa Aur, Fly, having been the first. She was in foal with him when Patsy bought her and her second, Smokey, had been carefully bred in the hope of his being a hopeful competition horse.

She always preferred to foal out of doors and when she was due Patsy and Katy took turns to check her before going to bed and at first light. Mack had offered to take turns as well but Patsy enjoyed these walks across the yard and the slight tension of anticipation until she saw the mare. She expected it would either be in the last few minutes of light that something happened, when the horizon was fading to dark from the colours of sunset, or in early morning with the light slowly growing and the birds still silent before the first colours crept up behind the hills. The horses, out all the time now, would often be lying down on their dawn naps and the air would taste of the day to come, sometimes still and clear with the promise of sun, on others alive with a rising breeze and the feel of rain in the air. It was on one of these damp mornings that Patsy reached the gate to find Goldie missing from the group of already grazing horses and knew that there would be news. She was right.

The foal was a colt, bay, like his marauding father, on his feet and sucking strongly. His mother pricked her ears as she saw Patsy approaching and her nostrils quivered with a deep, soft greeting.

'He's beautiful,' Patsy told her. 'Well done.'

She went up to the mare and stroked her neck and the foal stopped sucking and came curiously to investigate her, accepting her as another part of this strange place into which he had suddenly arrived.

"The eternal miracle of new life," thought Patsy, something which was always amazing whether human or animal, and this one so perfect a part of the damp spring morning.

Goldie followed as she walked back to the gate, the foal close beside her, and Lad and Boy came to meet them, warned by Goldie's flattening ears to keep their distance. Patsy unhooked a head collar from the gate and took mother and new arrival in for Goldie to have a well-earned scoop of feed and give her a chance for a closer look at the foal.

For a mistake he looked good, alert and well put together with the fine look of the Welsh breed.

Katy said that he should be called 'Mistake,' and Patsy had a feeling that the name would stick. Myra, admiring him when she and Verity brought their horses in to ride, said that seeing such a young foal was a real bonus to their holiday. They would be going home at the end of this, their second week.

'Rhianne said there's an agricultural show tomorrow,' she said. 'John's entered his ram and she said there are horse classes. She says it's a really nice sample of a Welsh country show. We'd like to have a look.'

'Why not?' Patsy thought it a good idea, and when she mentioned it to Katy she instantly said she could take a horse.

'There are in hand classes,' she said. 'I could take Smokey for the young hunter class. It's time he saw a bit of life. It's a nice friendly show and they always take entries on the day. I didn't think we'd have time to go this year with the visitors but it would be fun.'

It turned into a full-scale outing. Buzz was to go as company in the box for the young horse and Gareth was going with the ram and bringing Ethan with him. Mack liked the idea of a day out and Forrest said that Ana had some of her honey entered in the produce class. Rhianne and Patsy would both bring food and a variety of chairs and Rhianne welcomed the idea of another attraction for her visitors as these shows were quite frequent in the area.

The morning was sunny, with a feel of warmth in the

air, and it was quite a procession when they got on the road. Patsy was leading in the lorry with Smoky and Buzz in the back and Katy and Mack beside her with Tomos in his baby seat between them. Thinking that it would be useful transport for him Patsy had included Buzz's saddle in their load. Muff watched them go regretfully and Katy said it was a shame there was no class for mules.

Gareth drove the farm Land Rover towing the trailer with the trimmed and washed ram inside, and Rhianne had her car with John beside her, the visitors in the back, and the picnic stowed in the boot.

The show was held over several fields recently cut for silage. Rhianne drove towards the horse rings to find a good spot for watching while Gareth headed for the sheep pens with the ram and Patsy drove into the horse box park.

Smokey had been shown in hand before with his mother and foster brother and he bounced cheerfully out of the lorry with Katy and Buzz trundled down with Patsy. For years he and his late companion Harley had travelled shows and fetes with their old owner giving rides to children and the old donkey obviously remembered. He gazed around with pricked ears as if looking for something and then proceeded to bray, sending nearby horses into fits of snorting and prancing except for those who had met donkeys before. Katy, tying Smokey to the lorry, looked at him sadly.

'He's looking for Harley,' she said. 'I don't suppose he's ever been to a show without her.'

Patsy suspected that she was right. The two donkeys had worked the local events together for many years with Ethan's old employer. Mack had lifted Tomos down from the cab and now the little boy ran to hug Buzz who nuzzled him in what looked like relief.

'He thinks that's what he's here for, to give rides,' said Katy, and Patsy said that she would saddle him and Tomos could ride him down to watch Smokey's class.

'Better not bring him too close, though,' said Katy. 'Or we'll have half the class taking off in horror.'

She was starting to give Smokey a final polish before his class and Patsy saddled Buzz. With Tomos on board she and Mack followed the young horse towards the ring. There was soon plenty of attention.

'Are you giving rides?' several people asked, and when they found Rhianne camped at the ringside with her visitors Buzz was the centre of attention from hopeful children. Patsy lifted Tomas down for him to greet his guardian sheep dog and Buzz happily accepted pats and titbits from small fans. Patsy was still dealing with this when Gareth arrived to watch Katy's class and brought Ethan with him. Ethan's wrist was almost healed although he had been warned not to put any strain on it.

Buzz greeted Ethan with a half honk, his form of greeting, and Patsy knew that the donkey had expected him to be there as he always used to be at events. She handed him the reins and accepted one of Rhianne's chairs from which to watch Smokey's class. There were some nice young horses in the ring including one from a well-known local breeder, but

Katy's grey horse was not outclassed. He behaved well, striding out in a nice walk on a long rein, coming round in a nicely balanced turn, and trotting out with arched neck and free, straight strides. The judge was obviously impressed, watching closely and commenting to her steward, and Patsy was pleased but not surprised when he was brought out of line at the end and placed first.

Angie Shaw, owner of the stallion who had sired him, had been watching as well and came to congratulate them.

'My Jacaranda and your mare have done a great job,' she said. 'I look forward to seeing him under saddle next season.'

Patsy thanked her. Mack and John also said, 'Well done,' to Katy before going off together to share drinks in the bar tent and go to check on the ram's progress. Watching them go Angie grinned.

'I hear your husband has taken on that weird livery of Iris's,' she said. 'How is he getting on with it?'

'Very well,' Patsy was surprised. 'You know it, then?'

'Aries? Yes, I know it, or know of it, anyway' she said. 'Poor Iris, she really got had over that. I think she took the chap that owned it a bit too seriously and in the end he ran for it. Surprised he left the horse behind, he sounded pretty fond of it.'

'He didn't pay the livery though,' Patsy pointed out. 'That's how Mack got him.'

'I think she thought they had an understanding about that,' said Angie. 'But then something went wrong, something about smuggling, I understood.'

'That's what's we thought,' agreed Patsy. 'But it seems to have turned out well for us. Mack's quite happy with the horse, he seems a one off, as Jim the farrier, said.'

'Like Van, Giovanie, was, by all accounts,' said Angie. 'Although I never met him. Anyway, good luck with him, and more praise for Smokey. I reckon he and your daughter could have a great future together. My Jac's getting some great stock.'

'Are you busy this season?' Patsy asked her, and Angie nodded.

'Very,' she said. 'Mares in to foal and be covered again, liveries wanting trimming for shows, I've three here today for young stock classes.'

'I hope you've got some good help,' Patsy told her.

'That's one of the pressures,' Angie was letting Smokey lick her hand. 'My girl is off breeding herself, goodness knows if she'll be back after the baby, there's just me and my over worked head girl. If you hear of anyone who might fill in do let me know. I wouldn't mind a serious student wanting a career in stud work.'

Patsy promised that she would and Angie patted Smokey before hurrying off to supervise a horse she had in the next class and Katy grinned.

'That Van must have been quite something by the sound of it,' she said. 'Intrepid rider, seducer, smuggler...sounds like one of Mack's characters. Shame we'll never meet him.'

Patsy felt that it was perhaps a good thing for all of their peace that this was unlikely.

John's Dorset Downs ram won his class for

endangered breeds and the visitors went to explore the less horsey parts of the show, the sheep and cattle, the produce tents and the stalls.

'It's such a friendly show,' said Myra later, when they had gathered with Rhianne near the ring again. 'Agricultural shows in the south of England are so big and commercial.'

Remembering them from her days there Patsy agreed with her. This smaller scale show was a real family affair with everyone meeting friends and nothing too high powered about the competition. Later in the season shows did become more impressive but these early ones were friendly, warm up type affairs where young animals gained experience.

Ana's honey won an award and Forrest, joining them, said that she had received several orders for jars of it. He also said that his mother wanted to know if there was any improvement in the cottage atmosphere and Patsy promised to check it when they got home.

The show ground was beginning to empty now as animals were loaded and stalls sold out and it was time to go. Buzz, happily stuffed with titbits and his coat ruffled by many stroking hands, led the way into the lorry and Smokey clattered in behind. Myra said that they had enjoyed it. It seemed that the holiday venture was off to a good start.

CHAPTER SEVEN

It was not until next morning that Patsy walked down to the farm with some of the flowers which Ana had suggested for the cottage. The weather had changed, turning grey and cool and very still, what she thought of as nothing weather, no sun, no rain, no breeze, as if it had been turned to neutral, and that was how the cottage felt when she let herself in. Work on it was still suspended as they waited for an order to arrive from the builder's merchants and Forrest and Al were spending a day working on their own house at the eco village. There was the faint scent of Ana's herbs but the contents of one bowl had been scattered on the kitchen table beside it and Patsy suspected that a mouse had been at work.

She had brought a vase with her and she brushed the herbs back into their bowl and filled the vase with water. It was completely silent in the cottage and Patsy found herself hurrying. She was glad to
open the door again and feel a faint breeze and see Ethan coming towards her.

'I saw you go in, wondered if you wanted any help', he said. 'I was just filling the yard trough for the sheep that's in there.'

'Thanks,' Patsy took a breath of the sweet air and Ethan grinned.

'Funny feeling in there,' he said. 'And funny things happened, like me falling off that ladder. I was that sure I'd got it fixed safe.'

'How's your wrist doing?' Patsy asked him, and Ethan said 'Alright, but it's that boring, not being able to do things like handling the sheep and hitching up the trailer. Glad of my phone, I can do games on it and talk to people.'

'Have you spoken to Summer lately?' Patsy asked him. Ethan nodded.

'That Tabitha is nagging her,' he said. 'Always on about what she's going to do at Uni, what sort of career she'll be working for, Summer doesn't know, only things she really likes is animals. She doesn't even want to go to uni anymore. She's getting really hacked off with Tabitha.'

'Couldn't she take a gap year?' asked Patsy. 'Perhaps try a few things or travel a bit?'

It was what Katy had done before uni and a course in computer studies which had led to her present job. She and a friend had worked their way round much of Europe, funding it with casual work as they went.

'She'd like to do that,' said Ethan. 'A job, anyway. There was one at a donkey sanctuary, part time, but Tabitha, she said it was a sentimental waste of time. Summer reckons Tabitha just wants her safely out of her way.'

Patsy felt sorry for her. It could not be easy, living with the stormy progress of Tabitha and Flynn's marriage.

University did sound the best thing but it would only help if she wanted to be there, otherwise it might feel more like banishment.

The following day was Myra and Verity's last before going home. Verity wanted another beach ride and Patsy suggested going to Poppet sands on the opposite side of the creek to Cardigan. It

meant another trip in the lorries but Verity said another gallop on a beach would be worth it although her mother would have liked to ride on the hills. However Verity had her way. Katy regretfully said she must work and Gareth said he would take Tomos to the farm with him.

Mack, however, did come, saying that another beach ride on Aries was too inviting to miss.

Poppet sands stretched from the cliffs which were the starting point of the Pembrokeshire coast path down in a curve to the estuary of the river. There was a large area of sand dunes along the side of it, backed by marsh where ditches filled with water at high tide. Further in land the marshes became a nature reserve for birds and otters and a small herd of water buffalo had been imported to keep some of the watery growth in check. Patsy preferred the more open and rural feel of Newport but Poppet was an interesting landscape even if more of a resort with its lifeboat museum and popular cafe.

The horses liked the look of the sand. It was another fine day although it looked breezy out to sea with white foam cresting some of the rollers and a couple of fishing boats tossing quite noticeably as it met them.

They trotted and later galloped and then rode down to the edge of the estuary where the just turning incoming tide met the river current. The water looked quite shallow here and they splashed along the edge. The outlying streets of Cardigan looked quite close and Mack said that there was said to be a fordable crossing place somewhere. He did not add that someone trying to cross on horseback had been drowned there not too long before.

They let the horses paddle and paw the water and Patsy suddenly realised that Challenger was furthest out and Verity was having trouble persuading him to turn in the increasing pressure of water from the meeting of the two currents.

'Verity, turn him to the right,' Patsy called to her, but at that moment a long strand of weed wrapped around the horse's legs and Challenger panicked. A startled, plunging leap through the water took them further out and Myra gasped. They were obviously in trouble now, the horse still on his feet although the water was slightly less deep but moving strongly almost up to his stomach and Patsy suspected that they had found the ford. The feel of still solid ground under his feet was tempting Challenger to keep going forward rather than agreeing to turn. Mack realised it too and as the show jumper followed his instinct to jump out of trouble and landed even further out he sent Aries plunging after after him.

Myra gasped again and Patsy remembered the boys at Newport Beach saying that Van used to swim his horse quite far out. Challenger was off the solid ground now, splashing wildly as he found himself forced to swim. Patsy knew that all horses could swim but Verity's horse, at the moment, looked unconvinced of that. Both horses were swimming now and Mack was reaching for Challenger's rein and using Aries weight against the other horse's shoulder to force him to turn. There was a moment while it did not look as if it would work and Patsy had a horrible vision of both horses being swept out to sea, but then Aries's understanding of swimming began to give Challenger confidence and suddenly both horses found their footing on the causeway again and were plunging back onto dry ground.

'Thank goodness,' breathed Myra, and Patsy seconded that.

Both the horses were snorting and shaking themselves and Verity wailed 'My tack…look at my saddle.'

'You're lucky it's all you have to worry about,' Myra told her sharply. 'Why on earth did you let him go in so far?'

'I…I didn't notice,' Verity was sounding shaky now and Mack said, 'Good thing Italy here is a good swimmer.'

'He deserves a life savers certificate,' Patsy told him. 'And you. Are you alright?'

She thought Mack sounded a bit shaken himself but he just said 'Wet, but still breathing. Nothing like an impromptu bathe.'

'Let's get back to the lorries,' Myra looked at Mack.'I

can't thank you enough,' she said. 'If you and your brilliant horse hadn't been able to cope I dread to imagine what could have happened.'

'All in the holiday booking,' said Mack lightly. 'Life saving provided. Come on, we can trot them back and get home to hosepipes for these two and baths for humans. Oh, and maybe a brandy for humans and a full can of saddle conditioner for tack.'

The horses unsaddled and ready to load Mack gave Aries's ears a gentle pull and the horse rubbed his head affectionately against him.

'That Van must have had quite a relationship with this fellow,' said Mack thoughtfully. 'It's odd that he abandoned him as Iris said. I reckon we didn't get the full story.'

Patsy agreed. She also knew that they really had been seriously lucky, Mack's confidently bold horse had saved them from a serious conclusion.

Katy was in the yard when they got back watching Forrest lead Nell round the school with Brooke on his back.

'She just turned up,' she told Patsy. 'Then Forrest came back from the farm and found her playing with Muff and she begged him to give her a ride. Gareth had brought Tomos home, and he wanted his lunch, so I left them to it. Nell seems to think she belongs to him anyway.'

Nell certainly looked happy enough walking round the school with Forrest at her head and Brooke smiling in the saddle and Patsy could see in her the glory of all young girls smitten with ponies and knew that she could not object.

'Why isn't Forrest working?' she asked and Katy grimaced.

'Don't ask,' she said. 'More setbacks. A join in a new waste pipe in the kitchen hadn't been fixed firmly enough and it came apart when Al turned the tap on and started scrubbing some brushes. By the time he realised his feet were getting wet he had a flood and Forrest had to stop painting while his dad rolled the new Lino back and the floor dried out. What on earth happened to those two, serious swimming?'

Patsy explained and Katy was suitably impressed by the story and, like Mack, she said it was surprising that the horse's previous owner had left him behind.

'Something to do with Iris,' she said, and Patsy nodded.

'That's what we suspect,' she said. 'But lucky for Mack. However well Ana's paste works Osbourne isn't getting any younger.'

Neither Aries nor Challenger seemed to have suffered from their swim. Myra and Verity were going home next morning and both said that they had really enjoyed their holiday.

'I'll tell all my friends about it,' Myra told Patsy. 'And put a recommendation in my riding club newsletter.'

Patsy thanked her and even Verity said she was sorry to be going. Patsy watched the trailer drive out and knew that she would miss Myra. It was one of the penalties of a holiday business, she supposed, brief friendships like this.

Osbourne was still sound next day but Ana's remedies

did not seem to have done a lot for the cottage. Al got a new joint for the waste pipe but the dried-out Lino refused to lie properly so that it had ripples across it and Gareth decided that it meant buying a new piece. The flowers that Patsy had brought were drooping already and the mice had been back at the herbs.

'Can we borrow one of your cats?' Rhianne asked Patsy. 'My old yard cat hates to be shut in, scrabble and yowl, he would, if I tried it, and I hate seeing mice die slowly in traps however John laughs at me.'

Patsy agreed. One of her cat's grown-up kittens was always happy indoors and she took him, protesting, down to the farm in a carrying basket pushed on Tomas's buggy.

'I'll just give him some food to settle him but not enough to stop him wanting to hunt,' she told Rhianne.

The cat did not want to come out of the carrier. He peered timidly out before retreating to the back and crouching down.

'Thinks he's at the vet's, look,' said Rhianne, and Patsy hoped that it was the explanation and not something less explicable. She reached in and pulled the cat out and when he tried to duck back in she closed the door. She had brought a pouch of the luxury treat food which all the cats liked and when he settled to eat it she and Rhianne went quickly out.

'Come in for a coffee,' invited Rhianne, and Patsy went with her into the comfortable old stone farmhouse.

'Our first visitors were all praise for their holiday,' Rhianne told her. 'Family coming in tomorrow have a

daughter hoping to ride. Your horses are a real draw. My John is feeling the benefit of having less of the heavy work, I was really thinking we'd be having to give up.'
Pasty was glad to hear it. There was a middle-aged couple in the pod in the field, there for the walking, if this second cottage let could get started she knew that the farms future would be secure.
Before going back up the field to her own house Patsy went past the cottage, hoping that the cat would have finished exploring and settled to hunt. Instead she saw him at once on the kitchen windowsill, pressed against the glass, and when he saw her he went up on his hind legs scrabbling at the glass, his mouth open in a call for help. Patsy knew that she could not ignore him.
He was there as she opened the door and out past her legs before she could stop him. There was a yellow puddle on the floor just inside and she knew that he must have been seriously unhappy to make a mistake like that. He was gone already, back across the field to home, sending a couple of pigeons clattering up from the grass. Inside the cottage, when Patsy found kitchen roll to use to mop up, there was a heaviness in the air which made her feel unwelcome and with a rustle a drooping rose head spilled onto the table. She was glad to retreat back into the breezy day outside.
Pausing to look back at it the cottage looked blankly un-inviting and Patsy knew that it was still far from being a happy place for holiday makers.
The cat had made it back home and was in the yard

having his ears washed by his mother. He eyed Patsy doubtfully and she said 'Alright, I understand. I won't take you back, maybe the mouse won't want to stay there either.'

Brooke was there again with Nell and said that her school had an inset day. Patsy decided not to inquire too closely and gave up the attempt to ignore her pleading looks and got the pony's tack. Since being ridden with the trusted Forrest at her head Nell was more confident and she circled the school quite happily with Brooke on her back and Patsy could see hope of her becoming a nice ride, perhaps even useful if she fully adjusted to accepting guidance to her blind side.

Rhianne's next holiday family arrived and again riding was a popular idea.

'The daughter, Becky, it is', Rhianne told Patsy. 'She's a good rider, her mother says, and she asked me to make sure she gets a lively pony. Reading between the lines I think she's a bit of a problem. She struck me as being a might spoiled but, fair play, I mustn't judge too quickly.'

'I wouldn't call either of our faithful trekking ponies lively,' said Katy, when Patsy told her this. 'But you can hardly put her on Fly.'

'She'll have to ride Cinders,' said Patsy. 'She can be nicely forward going when her rider wants it.'

Becky proved to be a rather sulky looking girl of thirteen with fair hair in a long plait. She was dressed in smart cream jodhpurs and an expensive looking casual riding top and she eyed the plain and sensible

Cinders scornfully.

'She doesn't look very fast,' she said. 'I usually ride a horse, a thoroughbred.'

'She is a good rider,' her mother, an anxious looking lady wearing a blue track suit, told Patsy. 'We did promise her something as special as possible. After all, a holiday in Wales is a bit ordinary when her best friend is going to Greece but travelling is so unpredictable since these awful lockdowns.'

'Cinders is a nice pony,' Patsy told her, conscious of Katy rolling her eyes in the background as she led Golly out ready for Patsy. 'Ponies do get on better than most thoroughbreds in wild country.'

'It doesn't look very wild round here,' Becky sounded scornful. 'Nothing but fields and sheep,' but she stepped up to the pony, putting her hat on, and Patsy held Cinders for her to mount.

Becky sat well but she looked school taught, very correct with rather short reins. Cinders, used to more casual contact, was soon tossing her head.

'She likes a long rein,' Patsy told the girl. 'Horses need to be able to balance themselves and look around on the hills.'

'The horse I usually ride is very well schooled,' Becky sounded disapproving but she gave Cinders 's mouth another inch of rein and Patsy decided to leave it until she saw how they got on.

It was a breezy day with flying clouds and a few spatters of rain. The moor was looking very green on the open stretches and studded with gold in the gorse thickets. A pair of buzzards were soaring and crying their cat like calls. Patsy had decided to take Becky along the causeway and past the ruined farm. She intended to walk the first stretch while Becky got the feel of her mount but Becky was impatient.

'Can't we go faster?' she asked. 'I told Mum it would be boring.'

'Alright, but let Cinders pick her way,' Patsy warned her. 'She knows the rough patches.'

Surprised by sudden heels in her sides the grey pony jumped forward and came past Golly at a trot. Sighing, and hoping for the best, Patsy let Golly follow.

With Cinders in the lead they went onto the causeway but as they started up the hill Golly pricked his ears and his head went up. The moor ponies, set off by something or just ready to run, were coming over the crest, a sensible older mare in the lead followed by the rest of the group sent along by the feisty little grey stallion. Cinders had seen them too and as Patsy shouted a warning she turned back in front of them. Becky was tugging at the reins, suddenly alarmed, and Patsy swung Golly into the centre of the track. As Cinders came alongside Patsy grabbed her rein and the running ponies swerved round them. Golly stood his ground and the group went past and round them, the stallion pausing a moment to check them before going on himself.

'Loose horses on a bridle path,' Becky looked shaken. 'Surely it shouldn't be allowed?'

'This isn't really a bridle path,' Patsy told her. 'The grazing rights belong to the commoners, local farmers, who let us ride out here at our own risk from loose grazing stock.'

'Are there a lot of loose horses?' Becky no longer sounded scornfully confident and Patsy hoped that she was not going to raise doubts in the cottage log book or in the agency report about the riding being safe.

'Only the odd couple apart from that herd,' she assured the girl, and Becky looked relieved.

They had reached better ground now and Golly, anticipating the coming canter, began to jog.

'We can canter on up here,' Patsy told her. 'Just follow me.'

Golly jumped forward into his bouncy cob canter and Cinders, relaxing, came on behind. The breeze was cool in their faces, full of the moorland scents which Patsy loved, grass and herbs and newly springing bracken, mingled with warm horse and leather. A spatter of rain came on the breeze and the horses ducked their heads and turned their ears against it. It was enormously invigorating and as they reached the top and the path turned to follow the edge of the bracken plantation Golly slowed up and Cinders came alongside and Patsy was glad to see that Becky was smiling.

'Alright?' Patsy asked her, and Becky said 'That was fun, different to back home. We always ride on proper sand tracks on the common there.'

'Still different things to come,' Patsy told her. 'We turn down hill in a bit.'

'I have ridden downhill,' Becky sounded scornful again and Patsy said nothing. She had a feeling that her rider would not have been downhill like the coming bit at home in a tidy suburban park.

She was proved right. Becky eyed the steep stony path, hollowed out by horses and sheep and edged by steep, broken mud banks, dropping down steeply round the side of the bracken, and looked alarmed.

'Are we really going down there?' she asked.

'Just sit forward and loosen your reins,' Patsy told her. 'Cinders is used to it.'

Golly was already starting down, his weight back and hocks well under him, and Patsy heard Cinders start to follow.

'Keep your toes well in,' Patsy called back to her. The path was so deep that the rider's feet were well below the top of the banks and there was a risk of getting caught up. Behind her Patsy could hear Becky squeaking in what sounded like enjoyable alarm and she smiled to herself. Her rather scornful rider was finding that there were different kinds of riding to be enjoyed.

Gradually the path evened out and they followed it on between the bottom of the bracken thicket and the bog. The slender white bog cotton flowers trembled in the breeze and as they reached the grass where the path opened out a sky lark soared up from the rough land at the side, starting to sing as he lifted with the wind. There were options here, a twisty path through the heather or a straight green gallop to the gate. Cinders would stop at the end, Patsy decided to go for it and give her rider a thrill.

'We can let them go along here,' she said, as Golly

began to jog and the grey pony came alongside. 'Lean forward, keep a contact, and she'll slow up with Golly before the gate.'

'You mean, gallop?' Becky's face was alight. 'Oh...yes.'

Golly was off straight into his stride and Cinders went with him. Patsy checked that Becky was still looking secure and then leaned forward with her own horse. It was good going here and Patsy never lost the thrill of a real gallop, the feeling of suspension as the horse's strides blurred beneath her, the sweep of the wind in her face and the thud and splatter of hooves on wet ground. Beside her she could see Cinders ears turned back against the wind and Becky's enraptured face then they were through the gap between the sheep fields and both horses were slowing as the gate drew near.

'That was great,' Becky was patting the pony, still beaming. 'It's the fastest I've ever been. The riding school I go to doesn't like their horses to gallop.'

Becky's mother was waiting for them when they rode in, looking anxious, but she relaxed when she saw Becky's grin.

'I don't think I need to ask if you enjoyed that,' she said, and Becky assured her that she had.

She was eager to help unsaddle the pony and turn her out and while she was making friends with Muff and the donkeys her mother thanked Patsy.

'I was so afraid she was going to be disappointed in this holiday,' she said. 'My husband does get impatient when she plays up, but now, if she can have more rides to look forward to I hope it will be alright.'

She booked another ride for Becky in two days and Patsy hoped that the therapy would work. She could remember only too well similar problems herself when Katy was a stroppy thirteen-year-old and not helping Patsy to cope with her own difficulties with her first husband. Horses had helped then, Patsy had never regretted her determination not to give up owning them however hard it had sometimes been.

Back in the school Katy had brought Smokey and his foster brother in and after giving the grey youngster twenty minutes quiet riding in the school she was eager to make a start on the little mountain pony.

'If he's going to be ready for Tomos in a couple of years he needs to get started,' she told Patsy. 'And by the time Tomos grows out of him we can have Goldie's love child up and going.'

'That really is looking ahead,' Patsy told her, but however far off it seemed she knew how quickly time could pass.

"And I'm not getting any younger," she thought, with a sudden touch of fear. By the time Goldie's foster foal had matured, hopefully into a safe ride, who could know what that time might have brought for her and for Mack?

Suddenly in need of reassurance she said something to Katy about coffee and turned towards the house.

Mack was in the kitchen replenishing his coffee supply and Patsy felt a stupid sense of relief at the sight of him. They could still have years ahead of them if all went well but all the same she accepted the urge to touch him, almost like touching wood, and Mack looked round in surprise when she put her arms round him.

'Patsy?' He said. 'Everything all right?'

'Just checking in,' Patsy told him. 'Something Katy said about time. It made me think how quickly it can pass.'

'Patsy,' Mack kissed her and the brief moment of chill began to recede. Mack's hands and his mouth were warm and all this was still not very long discovered. Her response had Mack leaning back to look at her before taking her hand.

'I think we can do with a spot of privacy,' he said, and Patsy was laughing as he led her towards the stairs.

'Where were you?' By the time Patsy did go outside again Katy had turned Smokey out and was leading Lucky round the school in a saddle and bridle. 'He didn't mind tack at all and so I thought I'd carry on. And why have you got that sweater on back to front?'

'What...oh, I hadn't noticed,' she pulled at it, still feeling spacey after the immensely satisfying session with Mack, and Katy rolled her eyes.

'For goodness sake,' she said. 'You both act like a couple of teenagers. What had he done, got roused up with one of his randy characters?'

'Katy,' Patsy tried to sound offended but Katy was grinning, turning her attention back to the pony, and she decided to let it go. At least Katy had never appeared shocked by her and Mack's moments of unseemly behaviour. She dragged her attention fully back to concentrating on the pony.

Lucky was an obliging little character. Rescued from

the moor when they had found him beside his dead mother he had readily taken to being reared by Goldie alongside her natural son and he was turning out to be a typically attractive Welsh Mountain pony. It was easy to picture him in a few years with Tomos on his back in a first ridden class at a local show.

Tomos was certainly a keen rider already, thanks to Buzz, and after lunch Patsy walked down to Rhianne's with him on the gentle donkey. Buzz always took this duty seriously, walking beside her on a loose lead rein with happily pricked ears and a responsible expression. The fields were green, the horses in them peacefully grazing, the breeze had dropped to a gentle breath and summer was edging its way into the last of spring. Patsy felt a deep content, part of the peaceful day with her gentle donkey and her small grandson, her own body pleasurably relaxed, and she was not prepared for the sense of emergency that greeted them as they came through the gate into the yard. There was a blue BMW backed up to the cottage and a cross looking man with sandy hair and sober holiday clothes was lifting a crying Becky into it while her anxious mother and a concerned Rhianne looked on.

'What's happened?' Patsy felt her sense of peace rapidly departing.

'Becky's hurt her ankle,' her mother told Patsy. 'She went to have a look at the new cottage and managed to trip down the step coming out.'

'The door slammed, I told you,' Becky sounded hysterical. 'It just slammed...it isn't even windy. It was like being pushed and...and now I can't walk.'

She started sobbing again and the man, her father Patsy supposed, said 'Door should have been locked anyway if the workmen had gone. Looks like that's the end of this holiday. Come on Norah, let's get this child to a and e.'

He put Becky in the front seat and strapped her in, his wife got in the back and the car went off with a cross revving. Patsy and Rhianne looked at each other.

'That's one unhappy set of visitors, I'm thinking,' said Rhianne. 'Poor child will be getting blamed for it, and us, most likely, though there's no reason we should have been locking that door. It was only while Al went to the builders' merchants.'

'Except for what we know about the place.' Patsy was suddenly angry. 'But it's not fair, whatever happened in it is long over. Here, hold onto Buzz, it's time someone said so.'

'Patsy,' Rhianne was half laughing as she caught the donkey's rein. 'You aren't going in reading the riot act at a building, now is it?'

'Just watch me,' Patsy was already heading for the cottage. This whole business was getting out of hand and she remembered her own lingering angry ex-owner and his resentment of her when she first came to Bryn Uchaf. She and Emrys had eventually come to an understanding, maybe that was needed here.

Stepping angrily into the cottage Patsy was aware of a sense of something waiting, almost warily. The remains of the flowers had been cleared away but some of Ana's herbs remained in their dishes and she scooped them into her hand.

'What is it with you?' she demanded. 'We've tried, we've brought you amends, we've made you sound and offered you gratitude, whatever happened here is long over...we've left it behind, why can't you? Do you want to fall down into another abandoned ruin when you could be somewhere warm and happy?'

She paused for breath, realising that she must sound crazy, shouting at an empty building, but there was something here, an awareness, and she was sure that at least the sense of what she felt and was expressing was being absorbed.

'I'll bring you more herbs...fill you with flowers, prove you can be appreciated,' she looked round. The interior was almost finished now and Al's work had settled the window frames and the plastering, it could be as attractive as the other cottage if it would accept...accept what? Life...tenants, happiness... Patsy suddenly felt foolish. She wasn't living in some fairy tale, this was just an old building, a bit unfinished still, feeling a bit un-used, and incidents such as those here could happen anywhere.

"Just because there had been something left at Bryn Uchaf I'm imagining things," Patsy told herself, and she turned back to the door but before going back into the blooming summer she scattered the last of the herbs onto the cottage's new windowsill and when she touched the closed front door it swung open smoothly and silently to let her out. As she paused outside, conscious again of the sweetness of the day, it swung smoothly but somehow firmly closed behind her. Rhianne and the donkey were both watching as she emerged and Rhianne said rather hesitantly 'looking a bit pleased to see you go that seemed.' and Patsy knew that she was right.

It turned out that Becky's ankle was badly sprained but not broken which, as Rhianne said when she phoned Patsy, was a blessing but was hardly going to save the family's holiday.

'Trailing round the sights with a frustrated child on crutches won't be much fun, now,' she said. 'Maybe I should have my own say at that old building.'

She was half serious, Patsy could tell, but really, what use could it be apart from letting off their own frustration at the seeming bad intentions of what surely was really an insentient object?

Rhianne's fears for Becky's family holiday seemed justified when Forrest brought Buzz and his small rider home from the farm next day and reported that Becky and her parents had come back cross and frustrated from a trip to Tenby.

'Seems the girl couldn't manage her crutches on the sand and wouldn't try much anyway,' he told Patsy. 'Her Dad got cross and wants them to give up on the holiday and go home. He says he can't even sit outside and get to relax the way he'd been promised with Becky fidgeting and complaining.'

He lifted Tomos, protesting, down from Buzz's back and led the donkey to his field where Muff came eagerly to meet him. Once his friend was loose Muff bustled him off to play, prancing round him with her long white ears flapping and her ridiculous little tail in the air and in spite of the depressing news Patsy could not help laughing.

'It's a shame they haven't got anything like this to watch,' she said. 'Those two could keep anyone cheerful.'

"It could be an answer," she realised. "There was a small grassy enclosure beside the first cottage, and it would do Muff no harm to have a change of scene. She would suggest it to Rhianne."

Rhianne seized the idea gratefully. Although it was not their fault the disgruntled report of a spoiled holiday in the visitors' logbook would leave a sour taste apart from the fact that she would feel obliged to return some of their fee if they did cut their holiday short.

Muff was delighted with the outing. She left Nell without hesitating and gambolled down to the farm next day beside Buzz. She was halter broken now and Patsy led her while Gareth led his small son's transport. Left behind with Nell Jack called after them with a mournful bray but Buzz and Muff were not distracted and Patsy hardened her heart. They would be back later and the old donkey had Nell and the horses in the other fields for company while his daughter and his friend were away.

It seemed to work. Patsy left sliced carrots for Becky to give to the pair and told her that they were in her charge for the day. Her parents had comfortable garden chairs in the shade of the willow tree in the cottage garden close to them. Becky's mother had a book and her father was watching golf on an iPad. Luckily it was one of the first really fine, warm days of the summer with only a few puffs of white cloud over the green rise of the hills. With the animals to guard Becky was less frustrated by her ankle.

Outside the new cottage Al was back working on the cover of the drain from the waste which had cracked.

'Same problem as the sills,' he told Patsy. 'Whoever did this stonework got it set wrong.'

He had Ethan helping him and he would be there if Becky needed any help, and the holiday let seemed at least partially saved.

Back home Patsy had been planning to do some neglected jobs such as cleaning out her bantams and vacuuming through the house but Mack was outside with Aries and Lad in the stable keen to ride.

Tafarn-y-Bwlch,' he said. 'With a good long gallop and those long views of the sea. Just the day for it.'

It was infinitely more inviting than cleaning and Patsy remembered her determination not to waste the important times. Five minutes later she was on Lad riding up the road beside Mack and the eager liver chestnut horse with the rise of the seaward part of the Preselis ahead.

The track from the road and the cattle grid was wide and green and steadily rising towards the brilliant blue of the newly summer sky.

'Here we go,' Mack barely shortened his reins as they turned onto the sheep grazed turf and Patsy took a more careful hold of Lad's mouth as her eager little ex racer went with him. It was glorious, the speed and the vibrant feel of the keen horses, the green track flying under them and ahead the sense of approaching space as the track climbed into the sky.

'Steady,' Patsy sat back as they reached the top and beside her Mack's horse checked as he saw the land drop down ahead. There was the sea a few miles on and below them, three sides of white- speckled blue around the green of the hills, the scattered white and colours of the small farms and the darker edge of the small town.

'Perfect,' Mack brought Aries to a stop and they sat amid the steam of the blowing horses to drink in the view and breathe the sparkling air.

"He was right," thought Patsy, "How else could you describe it? A view like this made sense of things, a brief glimpse of something more, a sense of creation."

They sat and gazed as the horses breathing slowed and a flock of seagulls circled above them and Mack leaned down from his taller horse to catch her hand and kiss her. There was no need for words. Sitting upright again Mack let his horse walk on and as the track curved down they

rode on into the glory.

Having the animals to watch and connect with had certainly helped Becky and her parents. Although it was not quite the holiday that they had planned days relaxing in the luckily sunny weather and sightseeing in their car with the more cheerful Becky were making up for a lot. Muff's daily visits

gave Becky a focus and even her grumpy father had to smile at the little mule's antics. Patsy brought Cinders to the farm as well and with her ankle secure in its support bandage her parents agreed to let her ride the pony with Patsy leading her.

'Go a bit further,' suggested Mack. 'Get Mum and Dad on horses as well, suggest an expedition, you could go round the bridle path and cross over to show them the monster's grave.'

Patsy decided to suggest this and was surprised when Becky's Mum, who by now had become Lyn, was immediately enthusiastic. Her husband, rather grudgingly now answering to 'Geoff,' was less keen but gruffly agreed to come on foot. Katy would walk with Lyn on Sweep and Mack said he would keep Geoff company on foot. Lyn, it turned out, had ridden a little as a child and she

settled quite happily into the black pony's saddle.

They set out down the lane and turned into the bridle way which would bring them out close to the gate onto the moor. The way led between banks topped by hedges and a tangle of climbing growth, wild roses and honeysuckle, columbine and bramble. Cow parsley flowered below them, its lacy white flowers lively with bees, and the sunlight came in swinging shadows across the path ahead. The warm, scented air tasted of summer and even Geoff's discontented expression relaxed. The ponies walked calmly, ears twitching back and forward, quite content to be led from the ground,

and both the riders looked happy.

They came to the end of the path and crossed the road to the moor gate. Suddenly they were in a different world, out on the moor the view stretched away, brown and green, patched with stones and wet areas of bog, and the air smelled of damp ground, space, and a hint of sheep. The hill rose steeply into the sky and buzzards and a red kite soared overhead. Lyn took a deep breath, gazing round at the wild scenery, and behind the ponies Mack and Geoff were discussing England's chances in the current test match. A short stretch of rough ground brought them to the monster's grave, and as usual the ponies eyed it with slight wariness.

The so-called monsters grave was a low cromlech, two lines of inward curving stones divided by slightly rising grassy ground. The legend was that a water monster which had been terrorising the nearby settlement of Brynberian had been lured into capture by a tempting maiden and had been killed and buried there, the more likely story described it as an ancient burial mound. Whichever was true the horses, including the free roaming mountain ponies, seemed to avoid it, although one abandoned pony whom Patsy had rescued had found some shelter on it. Looking at it now Lyn shivered.

'It's a bit creepy,' she said. 'We had a look at the famous cromlech, Pentre Ifan, and I wasn't too keen on that, although the views were beautiful.'

'They're both just old stones,' Geoff sounded dismissive. 'The rest's imagination, isn't that so Mack?'

'I think there's a bit more to them than that,' Mack told him, but Geoff was clearly not convinced.

Becky was looking longingly at the hills and now she said 'My stupid ankle, I wanted to have another gallop and go up high. I wish I'd never gone to look at that spooky cottage.'

'Too much imagination again,' said her father, and Lyn said 'never mind, this is fun. We don't do enough fun things as a family, so you got us this, thanks to Patsy and her daughter.'

'And we can go along the moor to home,' Patsy told her. 'Through the ford by the otter's pool, we might even see one.'

They didn't see an otter but the ford was bright with the water creaming away over the rocks a little further down and the ponies walked cheerfully over the plank bridge which was the alternative to getting wet feet and Becky seemed fairly satisfied. By the time they reached Bynn Uchaf Patsy's legs were aching and she was missing her usual equine transport but the reputation of the first holiday cottage seemed to have been saved.

CHAPTER EIGHT

Becky's family returned home and the next booking was from a middle aged couple who planned to walk the coast path in stages but would not want riding. The idea of a week without trekkers was quite welcome but there had been one special request this time, to bring a pet, this being a tortoise. 'Surely that doesn't mean any problem,' said Katy. 'It isn't likely to make a noise or chase the sheep,' but it seemed, there was one thing to consider, the security of the cottage garden.

'Apparently he's quite an explorer,' said Rhianne. 'Off to see the world unless all the fences meet the ground. Gareth's going to peg the wire mesh down and fix a log to swing under the gate.'

'But tortoises are so slow,' Katy didn't see the problem, but Rhianne said, 'Not that slow. I recall my friend had one, when we were at school. Surprising how quick they can get along.'

This proved to be true. The tortoise, George by name, arrived and was introduced to Patsy and Tomos, who had arrived as usual for his day with Rhianne. The tortoise's shell was coloured in patches of dark and lighter brown from under which he surveyed the world with bright little eyes in his dark scaly head. He had a purple ribbon tied round one hind leg and trailing behind him.

'That's to make him easier to find if he hides,' his owner told Tomos. 'He can be quite good at hiding in long grass or under things.'

She was a lively looking lady with grey hair tied back in a youthful knot.

'I'm Brenda,' she told them. 'My hubby is Rob. He got a bit tired of helping me to find George which is the reason for the ribbon.'

'Have you had him long?' Patsy asked her, and Brenda laughed.

'About forty years,' she said. 'George is eighty, he was given to me by an old lady who was going into care and so I became his career.'

'Eighty,' exclaimed Patsy. 'And we think our horses are old at twenty.'

'Tortoises can live to over a hundred,' Brenda told her.

Tomos was trying to stroke the tortoise's head but George retreated into his shell and his owner said 'He's a bit careful of his head but he likes his shell stroked. They have lots of feeling in their shells.'

Fascinated, Tomos crouched down, gently stroking the smooth, cool shell.

'Is it his house?' he asked, and Brenda said it was.

'So he always has shelter and a safe place to go,' she told him.

She put two crisp lettuce leaves down by the tortoise's head and George began happily to eat.

'He should be safe enough in this garden,' Brenda told

them. 'Even with us out on our walks. I've brought his box, he likes to sleep in there.'

Patsy promised to ask everyone to keep an eye open for wandering tortoises and picked Tomos up.

His snack finished George was trundling away surprisingly quickly to explore his new surroundings. The last glimpse they had as he went on his way was the purple ribbon being towed into the bushes.

Muff was not pleased to discover that she was going to lose her time at farm. She had

enjoyed going down there with Buzz and being spoiled with titbits and attention from Becky, and she complained loudly the next time she saw Patsy set off with Tomos and Buzz for his morning with Rhianne without her.

Patsy was only halfway there when she heard a scampering of feet behind her, Buzz turned his ears back to listen, and the little mule caught them up with a triumphant squawk in her squeaky voice.

Tomos giggled and Muff ran round them kicking up her heels.

'You're as bad as your mother,' Patsy told her. 'Neither of you can stay where you're put. There's no Becky there to spoil you today.'

Muff was unimpressed. She trotted on ahead of them and by the time Patsy and her charges caught up she had found Gareth and was snatching mouthfuls of hay from the rack in the sheep pen in which he and Ethan were trimming sheep's feet. They were all being watched benignly by three of Gareth's young sheep dogs.

'Let her stay,' Gareth told Patsy. 'She'll be alright with Buzz. I'll keep an eye on them, so will the dogs. They were fine last week.'

Patsy lifted Tomos down and Bran came as usual to meet him followed by Rhianne. Gareth said he would bring everyone home when he was free.

Patsy asked how the building was going on and Rhianne said that Al had found another problem with the drain and had taken Forrest with him to buy pipes and cement.

'Always something with that place,' she said. 'Al said something about stone again but I don't see what that has to do with it. It does seem John was right about it, though fair play, we could have had problems with any site.'

Patsy left them to it. She had jobs to be done waiting at home and there were things she needed from the shops. She left the two friends nibbling grass in the small enclosure and walked back up the fields to home. It was warm today, but there was a heaviness in the air and a hint of cloud building over the hills. If it did rain Tomos would have to come home by car and his four-legged transport and his friend would have to come home separately.

It did rain. By lunch time heavy, thundery showers were sweeping down from the hill on a gusty westerly wind and in the fields the horses were sheltering. Arriving home from shopping Patsy was hauling bags in from the car when Rhianne drove in to deliver Tomos home complaining at missing his ride.

'Gareth said he'd bring the donkeys home later,'

Rhianne told Patsy. 'And Al said he'd give working outside a miss this afternoon, taken himself and Forrest home, hasn't he? Disheartening, I think he's finding these setbacks to be.'

They certainly were, thought Patsy, as she hurried Tomos to Katy's cottage. There had been no hold ups like these when her own old stables were turned into this cottage, or with the first of Rhianne's two.

It was a couple of hours later when Patsy, dozing by the Rayburn after lunch with a cat on her knee, heard something drive clattering into the yard and Buzz braying as it stopped. It was still raining, another thunder shower rumbling down from the hills, and rain was driving against the window.

Before she could reach the door it swung open and a drenched Gareth put his head in.

'What...' Patsy began, but Gareth, sounding unusually rattled, was already talking. Patsy gathered that something had happened to Muff. She scrambled into her jacket, hearing Buzz revving up for another burst of braying, and she saw John's sheep trailer in the yard hitched to the farm quad bike

Gareth was already outside again, lowering the ramp, and Buzz skidded out, followed by a weak squawk from inside. When she got there Patsy saw a soaked little white head and long, drooping ears partly raised from a bed of straw. Muff was wrapped in an old blanket and there was blood on one hind leg which was sticking out.

'Oh, poor Muff. What on earth happened?' Patsy was

beside her, stroking an ear, and Buzz scrambled back in and came to stand beside her.

'That damn cottage again,' said Gareth.' Al had left an old door over that collapsed drain and the new pit they'd dug for it. She'd slipped out of that bit we had them shut in and went exploring. Whole thing tipped when she trod on it and she fell in. Full of water, it was, by the time the old donkey raised the alarm with his braying. When Dad and me got there she was half drowned.'

'Let's get her in the stable,' Patsy could feel Muff shaking. Katy and Mack, both alerted by the noise, had joined them, and Mack said, 'We'll carry her in, give me a hand Gareth.'

He pushed Buzz out of the way, bending double to get inside the trailer and Patsy crushed herself back into the corner while they carefully lifted the little creature and her blanket and carried her out. The rain suddenly stopped as if switched off and a shaft of sunlight cut through the cloud. There were beds down in the boxes and Mack laid Muff gently down as an anxious Buzz crowded in behind them. Patsy knelt down and began carefully unwrapping her.

The little mule was a sorry sight, still soaked and plastered in mud, shivering, and with a nasty cut on her hind leg above the stifle.

'Mum saved her,' said Gareth. 'Not breathing, she was, when we got her out. Mum got her mouth open and cleared some mud out and massaged her and she started coughing and got her lungs working.'

Buzz was licking Muff now, making a wheezy

coughing sound himself in donkey talk, and Muff responded by getting her front legs out in front of her and sitting up.

'Shall I get her mother?' asked Katy, but Patsy said she thought Buzz was doing the best job possible.

'We need the vet, though,' she said. 'There must be a risk of pneumonia and that cut looks nasty.'

'She needs to get warm too, as fast as possible,' Mack looked round the barn. 'You had a heat lamp when your sheep were lambing. Is it still here?'

'It's in the tack room,' Patsy told him, and he went to fetch it while Katy, hearing Tomos shouting in her cottage, rushed guiltily off to fetch him.

With the hanging lamp above her Patsy and Buzz worked on drying Muff while Gareth said he had to get back to help his father and Katy took Tomos indoors. Mack stayed, taking turns with the drying, and gradually Muff stopped shivering and ate a few mouthfuls of a warm mash which Katy had mixed for her. By the time the vet arrived Muff was on her feet, shaky but warmer, and he listened to her chest and said that there was still some congestion in her lungs.

'I'll give her an anti-congestion jab and an antibiotic,' he told them. 'Keep her in and warm, she can do without another soaking and there are more showers about. This donkey's got the right idea about massage.'

He patted Buzz, who was still eager to keep licking his small friend. Muff's cut was still bleeding and the vet cleaned it well and inserted a couple of stitches.

'Give me a ring if she starts to run a fever,' he told

them. 'And keep an eye on her. She's pretty shocked. Great little creature, my wife and I both enjoyed her video.'

He gave Buzz's neck a scratch and told him to keep up the good work before he drove off. Patsy said that she would stay with them and Mack volunteered to make them sandwiches. Rhianne phoned to ask how Muff was.

'If we hadn't laid out a good bit on that cottage we'd think again,' she said, 'I was never much of a believer in ill wishing and such but this is getting to me, Geraint and Ethan, Becky, all the setbacks, that Ana's talk, and now your poor little mule.'

Pasty agreed with her. It did seem that in spite of her outburst to it something more than coincidence was still having an effect. Even Al thought so.

'I told Ana about it,' he said. 'There's something I found that might give her an idea.'

Muff seemed quiet but comfortable that evening and Patsy brought Nell in for the night as company. Buzz would have stayed but Jack was missing him. Patsy went out to check her at four in the morning, said to be the critical moment of the night, a time for births and also for deaths. The showers had stopped and the sky was clear and calm, the first pale light fading the stars over the dark rise of the hills. Muff was asleep, stretched out in the deep shavings with Nell dozing on her feet beside her. Her breathing looked normal and all seemed well. Patsy paused on her way back to bed to watch the pink promise of dawn. It seemed the usual miracle, the return of the light, the first stirring of the birds, the familiar shapes of day emerging from the dark. For a moment she felt in awe of it, of how little humanity really understood of the reason for it all and what life and time were really about. Then the first blackbird of the day clattered out of the hedge and one of the cats twined around her ankle and she shook herself back to attention and went into the house and back for a last couple of hours in her warm bed beside Mack's warm sleeping body.

Muff seemed to have got away with her brush with death. She was awake but subdued later when Patsy went out again and found Katy feeding them all. It was warmer today, and at the gate Buzz was waiting for his self-appointed charge. Muff came rathe cautiously across the yard with Nell but once loose she tried a little skip before going off with Buzz to a sunny corner. Patsy was about to go in when the cattle grid rattled and Ana peddled into the yard.

'Al told me he found something,' she said. 'And I thought I'd find out first how much more damage there'd been. How is the little creature?'

Buzz came to the gate when Patsy called him and Muff came with him. Ana laid a gentle hand on her head and Muff leaned into it, half closing her eyes, and for a minute or so they stood like that before Ana said, 'She has a very strong life force, I think she'll be alright.'

'I hope so,' Patsy was sceptical although there was something very convincing about Ana, who now gave Muff a gentle pat before turning back to Patsy.

'Now to see what it is that Al's found,' she said.

Patsy was curious about that as well and Ana left her

bike by the block and they started down the fields together. As they came level with the remains of Mary's cottage Ana paused.

'There is a very strong presence here,' she said. 'Someone seeing once lived nearby. Do you know who it was?'

'Mary,' Patsy was startled. She wasn't sure if Forrest knew the story of the old wise woman, but could Ana really be sensing vibes from her? She decided not to question. Ana nodded and walked on.

'I think she was a special person,' she said. 'Very different to what I feel at this next site.'

That was true anyway, thought Patsy. She was becoming impressed by Ana. Either she was very convincing or she really was a true sensitive.

Al was expecting them. He and Forrest were at work on a replacement pipe in the now cleared out pit at the cottage door and he hauled himself out and rubbed his hands on a muddy towel.

'It's on the sill there,' he said, nodding to the window, and Patsy saw what looked like an odd shaped stone. Ana picked it up as though it was hot, handling it carefully, and Patsy saw that there was a hole in it, firmly packed with clay.

'What is it?' she asked, and Ana asked Al 'where did you find it?'

'Under the door stone,' Al told her. 'Been there a pretty long while by the look of it. I only found it as rescuing the little mule meant lifting that old doorstep.'

'It's a hag stone,' Ana explained. 'A stone with a hole right through it, a good luck symbol for a person who finds one, the luck and protection flow through the hole, but this has been filled in deliberately. It would stop the luck, and close in bad feelings. I've never seen one used that way before but I think this one was.'

'So it could keep in resentment, in a place?' Patsy felt her skin prickle and Ana nodded.

'I think that was the reason,' she said. 'Burying it under the entrance would hold the influence inside. Someone must have had a strong reason to put a jinx on the place.'

'And if Muff hadn't gone exploring we'd never have found it,' said Patsy.

'You seem to have got your own protection there,' Ana sounded serious. 'A white animal, often connected with good fortune. Al, have you got a long nail or something I can chip this out with?'

Al produced a strong six-inch nail and Ana began gently to pry the solid clay out of the hole in the irregular shaped grey stone. Her long brown hair with the few touches of grey was only tied back loosely today and she was wearing a green smock in some material which shimmered slightly and clung around her. She looked slightly other worldly, almost fey, but verging on beautiful and Patsy saw Al watching her in a way that clearly showed his feelings towards her.

The last of the clay dropped out of the hole and Ana looked round.

'It needs water,' she said. 'These stones were formed by water wearing the hole in them, on the beach or in a waterfall. Water will clear the way through.'

There was a tap by the yard gateway and Ana took

the stone to it and turned it on, flushing the water through the hole and ignoring the water splashing over her sandalled feet. Patsy could see that her mind was divorced from them, concentrating on what she was doing, and suspected that she was watching a genuine witch at work.

'Now it needs to go back in place,' Ana said. 'Over the door, perhaps, with a secure fixing.'

Al found wire and a large staple and Ana used his toolbox as a step to reach up and fix the stone in position, the wire through the hole. For a moment she stayed there, gazing at it, and then she stepped down and Patsy could see that she had returned to her more usual practical self.

'Now,' she said. 'We'll wait and see if things settle down.'

She gave Al a wifely kiss, hugged Forrest, who had been watching from a slight distance, and said that she would hurry back as she had a customer coming for honey. Al. watched her go before recovering his toolbox and starting to search for something and Patsy turned to look inquiringly at Forrest.

'Alright?' she asked him. He was looking somehow diminished but he nodded.

'It just gets me a bit when she goes sort of different,' he said. 'Leaf hates it, says Mum's just showing off, but it's not that. Brooke's a bit flaky too sometimes, but Dad says they're just wired a bit different.'

'Forrest, give me a hand, we need to get this pipe back in before it rains again,' Al told him. They got back to work and after watching for a moment Patsy stepped quietly past them into the cottage.

All seemed as usual. It was very still, outside there was quite a strong breeze blowing but there was no sound of it in here, just a feeling of emptiness. The remains of the herbs were still on the windowsill where she had scattered them and there was a slight scent of them in the air. Patsy realised that it was the feeling she had when entering a house when everyone had gone out.

'I'll come back later,' she told the stillness. 'Just...be at peace.'

Turning back she let herself out again into the warm, moving air and the sounds of sheep and of Al and Forrest filling in the hole. "She really would come back later," she thought. "Perhaps with some cheerful flowers."

Muff was still very quiet when they started the evening jobs and Patsy decided to bring her in for another night so that they could keep an eye on her.

'With Nell or Buzz?' wondered Katy, and Patsy decided on the old donkey. He was a far better nursemaid than Muff's flighty mother. Before feeding them Katy held Muff while Patsy took her temperature. It was slightly raised and she was not very interested in the little feed that Patsy had prepared for her.

'I'll have to get the vet back if she's no better tomorrow,' Patsy was not happy about the little mule. She had left the rest of her feed and gone back to lying in her favourite corner. Buzz finished the feed for her but he too seemed concerned, going to nuzzle her and then settling down to stand protectively beside her. It was obviously going to be a restless night for herself and Katy, Patsy knew.

Muff was still not right next morning. She was not very interested in food, chewing half-heartedly on a few strands of hay when Patsy held them for her. Outside the weather had settled, the sun was warm and in the hay fields the grass was tall and silvery with flower. Rather doubtfully Patsy decided that the sun would be good for her and led her out to her field with Buzz following anxiously behind. Nell greeted her daughter with an impatient push, almost as though she was telling her to snap out of it, but Muff went droopily with Buzz to a spot in some dappling shade.

'Vet again?' asked Katy, but Patsy was doubtful.

'Let's give her a bit longer,' she said. 'Her temperature's normal, perhaps she just needs time to get over the shock.'

Forrest came in later with Brooke, who said that she had a day off school as the teachers had a training day again.

'Dad doesn't need me until later,' Forrest told Patsy. 'I thought I could take Nell for a walk.'

'And with me riding her,' said Brooke hopefully, and Patsy agreed. These outings seemed to be good for the one-eyed pony who was certainly gaining confidence from them.

Ana had sent a herbal tonic for Muff and when Forrest and his sister had set off towards the stream Patsy looked at it rather doubtfully. How much of Ana's therapies would be too much, she wondered. She might be a witch but that didn't also make her a vet. On the other hand Osbourne was still sound. She decided to try it.

Muff also was doubtful at first when Patsy smeared a spoonful of the stuff onto her tongue but, as Osbourne had, she obviously liked the taste. Buzz sniffed at the spoon inquiringly and looked as though he would like a share but Patsy hastily took it away. She didn't want all her animals eating things of which the vet, and possibly the law, would disapprove.

Whether from the paste or her own resilience by lunch time Muff was beginning to look brighter. Remembering her promise to go back to the cottage Patsy raided the flower bed which Mack had included alongside his vegetables and picked a mixture of bright cottage garden flowers,

lupins and giant daisies and two spikes of red gladioli. Seeing her with them as she tied them together Mack laughed.

'It'll certainly brighten things up,' he said. 'Is this part of our witch's spell?'

'I read somewhere that after banishing a bad influence you shouldn't leave a blank,' Patsy knew that this had been at the back of her mind, gleaned from some book or film. 'Ana believes in the good of flowers, so I'll try it.'

Al and Forrest were at work on the repair to the new drainage and Patsy took her flowers into the house. She knew at once that something had changed, the empty feeling was replaced by the usual quiet coolness of any empty house. There were decorating materials in the kitchen, cans of paint and rolls of lining paper, and the scent of herbs hovered faintly among that of the work in progress. Patsy put fresh water in the vases and settled cheerful displays of her flowers in the living room and a bedroom.

'There,' she told the emptiness. 'Forget whatever was wrong here and accept a new start. This could be a happy house.'

She let herself back into the summer afternoon and glanced back. Was it her imagination or did the windows look less opaque, as though somewhere behind them light was creeping in.

By next day, thanks either to her own resilience or perhaps to Ana's tonic, Muff seemed back to normal. She played with Buzz and Gareth's young sheepdog and happily ate her food, and Forrest, coming to visit Nell after work, reported good progress with the cottage.

'It seems more comfortable in there,' he said. 'Even Dad thinks so. Leaf laughs at us, says it's nonsense though she's keen on the herbs and Mum's bees and the bantams she keeps. She just thinks the witchy stuff is rubbish.'

There was a different sort of emergency the following evening. evening. Brenda and Rob came home from their day on the coast path to find George had gone missing.

'There's a hole under the fence in the corner,' Brenda told Rhianne and Patsy, who had come to collect Tomas after she had been shopping. 'It looks as if something has been digging.'

'Rabbits,' said Rhianne. 'There's a nice bit of lettuce here, look, to tempt them, some your old boy must have missed.'

They searched, looking under bushes and stones and the back of the buildings in the yard, but there was no sign of the variegated shell and its occupant. Buzz and his inevitable white shadow, who had insisted on accompanying Patsy on her walk down, watched curiously. Brenda was becoming frantic at the thought of going home next day without him when Muff, bored now and finding some tasty thistles, picked something up, waving it, and Brenda exclaimed 'That's his ribbon...but where's George?'

It was Tomos, closest to the ground, who found him in the end, well hidden in a cool spot under the yard water trough. On hands and knees in the dust Brenda pulled him out while Patsy retrieved his ribbon from Muff.

'It seems to have frayed,' she said. 'It must have caught on something and come off his leg.'

'Thank goodness she's got the wretched creature,' Rob was handing his wife a lettuce leaf for the stray. 'We'd have had to camp here until she found it. Useful pair you've got there Mrs. Macintosh, boy and equine. We'd better get in now, got the packing to do, and that creature can stay inside until we go.'

Brenda held George for Tomos to stroke him and Muff, having given up her ribbon, proved her return to health by scampering across the yard. Brenda and Rob, with George safely held, went off to the cottage and Rhianne gave a sigh of relief.

'Another crisis averted,' she said. 'This holiday letting gives us some dramas, we'd best be hoping they all end so happily.'

CHAPTER NINE

Brooke had got on well riding Nell and Patsy gave her another lesson in the school. Nell's confidence. was growing all the time, she accepted Brooke's rein aid to turn to her blind side and she circled happily on both reins. Brooke's riding was coming on as well and they made a nice pair and Patsy felt that these sessions were good for both of them.

It was time again for Cardigan show, much bigger than the earlier show, with challenge cups and produce stalls, fairground rides and agricultural machinery displays. Fly, under his show name of Heddfa Aur, was entered in the class for cob stallions. Katy had Smokey in the young riding horse in hand class, John had a group of his Dorset Down sheep and his young ram in the sheep classes, and Rhianne had a fruit cake and a batch of Welsh cakes in the cookery classes. Forrest said that Ana had a stall selling herbs and honey and some knitted angora gloves and scarves.

'She'll have Leaf helping her,' he said. 'She's as keen on all that as mum is. Brooke thinks it's boring.'

The show day, as it often seemed to be for Cardigan, started wet, with a forecast of heavy thundery showers, but it had not affected attendance Patsy discovered as she took her place in the queue of cars and horse boxes heading for the show ground. Cattle and sheep were required to be on site. earlier and Gareth had gone with John but would be there to show Fly in hand. Katy and Mack were in the box beside her with an excited Tomos bouncing in his seat between them as they turned into the busy show ground.

Smokey's class came before Fly's and again Patsy thought that the young grey horse was outstanding. She was delighted to see that the judges agreed as he was called in first. Katy brought him out of the ring beaming and several people congratulated her.

'Next year I'll be riding him here,' she told Patsy. 'And maybe in the jumping.'

'If all goes well,' Patsy was more cautious but Katy refused to be dampened and Patsy hoped that she would be right. She could not help feeling that remarks like that, where horses were concerned, needed making with firmly crossed fingers.

There was no need for crossed fingers for Fly this year anyway. With Gareth at his head he trotted out with what Patsy thought of as all his flags flying in an impressive display. His bright coat shone in spite of the wet and he was called out first. The judge, who had seen him before, smiled and patted him and Fly shoved his nose against his shoulder.

'He said he thinks he gets better every time he judges him,' Gareth reported to Patsy, and Fly pricked his ears and looked smug.

There would be a wait now before the show

championships were judged between the winners of each group of classes.

Forrest and Brook had come to watch and Forrest said that Leaf was minding Ana's stall. They watched and helped load the horses for the wait and Mack bought hot, crisp newly fried doughnuts for everyone. The rain had stopped although there was still plenty of cloud and Patsy decided that the horses, loaded and settled with hay nets, could be left while they had a look round the show ground and watched Gareth's sheep dog demonstration.

There was a good audience for Gareth's sheep dog display. He had three dogs with him, two young ones whom he had trained, and a more experienced one. All three were the traditional old Welsh breed, collies, but with brown brindled coats instead of the more usual black and white colour. They were impressive workers, answering immediately to Gareth's commands and working as a team gathering, moving, and penning the little flock of Welsh mountain ewes. The sheep were spooky, disturbed by the strange surroundings of the show ground with its crowds and noise, but the dogs made no mistakes and there was a round of applause from the spectators, many of whom were quite knowledgeable. Patsy heard some complimentary remarks including one from a competent looking lady saying that she would contact Gareth about finding her a well-trained young dog.

John's ram had won its class and they headed back towards the lorry park past the trade stands and Ana's pitch. This was attractively laid out with a

background of plants, among them rosemary and thyme, assorted mints, blue leafed sage, and some less usual ones. The central display was of varied packets and jars of these and of prepared pastes and liquids and of pots of glowing golden honey and sections of bees-wax . It seemed to be doing good trade in the charge of a girl with long rich brown hair who looked sufficiently like Ana to be Leaf. Forrest introduced them and the girl grinned.
'The horse people with the haunted cottage,' she said clearly, and several people looked round. Forrest looked embarrassed.
'Cool it Leaf,' he said, and the girl looked innocent.
'True, isn't it?' she asked. 'Mum told me all about it, quite convincingly. I almost wanted to visit it.'
'Don't Leaf,' Brooke was glaring, but they were distracted by Ana's arrival carrying a wicker basket containing a large, very fluffy grey rabbit.
'Everything alright?' she asked. 'I love your cob Patsy, he must have a great chance of being champion. '
Patsy thanked her and Ana went behind the stall and put the rabbit in a safe corner. Distracted from the subject of the cottage Leaf pulled a handful of grass for him.
'He won his class,' Ana told them. 'Best Angora. He was only for sale because the owner needed some fresh blood and had bought a young buck. She'd seen some of my products and knew I'd make good use of his hair.'
'Mum makes things with Angora hair,' explained Brooke. 'She's got a flock of them, we all help comb

them out. People who are allergic to some wool can wear things made from angora.'

Pasty was impressed. There seemed to be no end to Ana's natural products.

The loudspeaker was warning that the judging and parade of champions would start in half an hour and they left Ana and headed back to the lorry park for their two horses. They paused in the walkway between that and the show ground to let a woman go through leading a large bay horse. She was good looking and impeccably turned out, dressed for showing in hand with a number round her waist and a showing cane in her hand, and Patsy realised that they had met before.

'Call me Iris,' she hissed at Mack, and saw that he too had recognised Aries seller. She had recognised them as well and she stopped the horse as they entered the lorry park and turned to greet them and Patsy noticed what looked like a flash of dismay as Mack said 'Hello. Iris, isn't it?'

'Mr. Mackintosh,' Iris sounded determinedly hearty. 'How is the horse? Not here today is he?'

'Not my sort of riding,' Mack told her. 'I'm enjoying the horse, though, had some lively rides on him.'

'You're really happy with him then?' Iris sounded almost disappointed. 'If you're not...well, I did rather rush you about him.'

'No, I really like him,' Mack assured her. 'Lucky for me the owner did abandon him.'

'Well, it really wasn't quite like that. Actually...'Iris was cut short by the bay horse making a dive out of the walkway towing her with him, and a large Shire horse coming behind him. Towed away towards the ring by her horse Iris gave them a half wave and gave up. Patsy grinned.

'It sounds as if she's having second thoughts about selling him on,' she said, and Mack agreed.

'Whatever her problem it's done,' he said. 'If she's really bothered she's got my phone number. It sounds as if something is making her feel guilty. I wonder what happened.'

'Probably best if we don't find out,' Patsy was hurrying now. 'She made the decision, and you've got a nice horse. Hang onto him.'

For the moment she had something else needing her attention.

There was no time to give Fly more than a quick wipe down before taking the eager chestnut to Gareth, who had left his dogs with his father and was waiting by the ring.

The champions from every in-hand class were heading there, show ponies, riding horses, cobs, Arabs, coloured horses and heavies. Fly loved the attention as they circled the ring while the judges watched and the spectators applauded and again Patsy was glad that it was Gareth at his head as the shining chestnut arched his neck and stepped eagerly out. It did not take long and there was an enthusiastic burst of applause as Heddfa Aur, the living illustration of his name of 'Golden Flight,' was called to stand regally in place as in hand show champion.

'He really is great,' Katy said afterwards. She had

been slightly disappointed not to get a championship place for Smokey but it was no disgrace not to have. 'I wonder if old Emrys can see him. His Highflyer certainly bred a real champion.'

'I hope he knows,' Patsy remembered something which seemed to be the essence of Emrys, previous owner of her home, helping with problems in Fly's foal hood. He might have resented her, a loan English woman, moving in, but that resentment had seemed to change to acceptance. Perhaps whatever was affecting Rhianne's cottage really would eventually do the same.

It certainly seemed hopeful. When Patsy, with Buzz's help, took Tomos to Rhianne next day she called in to check progress. There were cheerful sounds of activity, someone was using a drill, a radio was playing music, and her flowers were still bright and fresh in their vases. Al, looking quite secure up there, was on a step ladder fitting the top of a new door frame and Forrest was sweeping wood shavings into a pan. They both greeted her cheerfully and Al said 'Something's cleared the air in here up a bit anyway. It feels a lot more comfortable today.'

Patsy was very glad to hear it. Whatever Forrest and Leaf thought of their mother's methods it did seem that there was some truth in them.

CHAPTER TEN

Rhianne's dog walking visitors went home and her new visitors arrived, a family with three children, twin twelve year old girls and a boy of fourteen. The girls were pony mad and keen to ride but their brother was dismissive.

'Girls' stuff,' he said, when Rhianne brought them all down to see the horses. 'I used to like it but it was boring. Most men think so.'

'Not all of us,' Mack told him. 'Some of us have more sense. There's nothing boring about riding a good horse.'

'You write books, don't you?' The boy was eying him with sudden interest. 'Rhianne said. I've seen your picture on covers, you write those crazy fast thrillers about spies and chases.'

'You could call them that,' admitted Mack. 'I even had a horse chase with a killer in 'Wild Water.'

'I read that, it was great,' the boy looked impressed. 'The horse swam a river and saved the hero from being caught. Do you really ride like that?'

'Probably not quite,' Mack told him. 'Although my horses can swim.'

'I suppose riding can be exciting,' the boy glanced at his sisters who were grinning. 'The trotting round a school that these kids do sure isn't.'

'I think Patsy's rides are a lot more than that,' Mack told him. 'Come out on one and see.'

'Will you come?' he asked, and Mack agreed that he would.

As always with new customers Patsy had them in the school first to check their ability. She had the girls, Kylie and Kate, on the cobs and their brother Colin on Boy. The young pony was safe enough but he needed his rider to pay attention and if the boy found that he was not a plod it might make him take a proper interest.

All three proved competent enough, the girls happy on Cinders and Sweep, but Colin, obviously showing off, started by giving Boy a kick which sent him leaping forward and setting off at a canter which almost unseated his rider.

'Gently,' Patsy warned him, when he had got Boy walking again although looking startled. 'I thought you said riding was boring.'

The girls were laughing and Colin looked defiant.

'Well I suppose not always.' he said. 'But if it's just going round in circles it is.'

'Give it a chance,' Patsy told him. 'But you can't go out where we are about to unless you can stay on and have a bit of control. Now, try it gently, just a touch with your heels.'

A gentle touch was enough to send Boy hastily forward and Patsy kept them in the school until she was sure he had settled down. Mack had Golly and Osbourne saddled when they were ready to go out and a bit of Colin's scorn surfaced again when he saw Osbourne's plain and solid looks.

'That one doesn't look very exciting,' he said. 'Do you always ride him.?'

'Looks aren't everything,' Mack told him. 'They need brains as well out on our hills.'

Katy watched them set off looking envious. She had Tomos this morning as Rhianne was doing a supermarket run and also having her hair cut. Tomos was not pleased either, demanding his trip on Buzz to the farm, and Katy had to agree to taking him for a walk on the donkey before she tried to settle him with his toys while she attempted to do some work.

Patsy was determined to prove to Colin that riding need not be boring without taking any risks. A safe circuit on the lower slopes, she decided, ditches to scramble over, a deepish stream to ford, and a short stretch of open grass for a bit of speed. All the horses enjoyed this, hopping over the ditches, jumping the clear cut wider one, splashing happily through the ford and sending two ducks clattering noisily up from it. Coming through the gorse thicket to the open stretch Patsy warned them to sit tight. All the horses expected the coming gallop and were on their toes and she could see that Colin was going to get his thrill as Boy began to jog.

Coming out onto the green stretch Mack sent Osbourne away first to give a firm lead and Boy was close on his heels. Cinder and Sweep followed a little more sedately and Patsy let Golly follow them.

Colin was clearly not in much control, sitting back

and looking a bit startled, but the girls were leaning forward, laughing. Mack was steadying Osbourne as the open stretch narrowed back to a track through gorse bushes and Boy almost ran into his heels. Cinders and Sweep came to a more controlled pace behind them and Patsy followed as, steadied by Osbourne's solid quarters, they all got back into a trot.
'Everyone alright?' Patsy asked them, and the girls said, 'that was great.' Patsy looked at Colin who was flushed and breathless. She couldn't resist saying 'boring?'
'I only said what the girls usually do is boring,' Colin looked defensive. 'This is different.'
The girls were grinning and looking ready to mock him and Mack said 'Right, now to demonstrate my lad's brains a bit. Watch how he deals with gates.'
The gate off the moor had a tall bridleways' handle on the latch. Mack walked Osbourne up to it and dropped the reins onto his neck. Osbourne reached out to rub his neck on it, pushing it back, and then let the gate swing open so that Mack could catch it and they could go through.
'See what I mean?' Mack asked Colin, who could not help looking impressed.
'Alright,' he said.' I never knew horses could be that clever. How did you teach him to do that?'
'I didn't have to,' Mack told him. 'He just copied me.'
He steered Osbourne to one side while they went through and then turned him back and let him reach out his neck again and swing the gate back with a rub from his chin. The girls applauded and Colin was

clearly impressed.

'Can we ride again?' the girls wanted to know when they got back, and Kylie said 'Rhianne told us you sometimes ride on the beach. We'd love to do that.'

'Can we?' Kate was eager and even Colin said, 'I'd go with that.'

'We'd be too many to go down in the lorry,' Patsy told them. 'We'd have to ride down, it would mean an early start to get on the beach before horses are restricted for the busiest times.'

'We don't mind getting up early,' said Kylie, and even Colin agreed. 'Can we do that?' the suggestion was popular and Mack laughed.

'Looks as if it's settled, 'he said. 'I could bring Italy, it might be a bit hard on the old boy's joints.'

When she heard about the ride Katy said that she would come as well.

'I can ride Lad can't I?' she said, and Patsy rather doubtfully agreed. Her ex-racehorse was fairly sensible but he did love to gallop and the beach was very tempting. She would not like to see Lad start a real stampede.

Rhianne said that she would have Tomos early for the day and she would also supply a packed brunch for everyone which the parents, who wanted to watch, could drive down with and share.

Luckily the tide times were right for the day with the tide low early although the weather forecast did suggest showers.

'We'll get wet anyway charging along in the surf,' Katy pointed out.

'But we won't go swimming,' Patsy had not forgotten their last trip to the beach.

It was quite a cavalcade that set off just after the sweet summer daybreak down the stoney track through the ravine which was the shortest route to Newport. Patsy was in the lead on sensible Golly and Mack riding rear guard on Aries. Fly watched them go with a lordly shriek and Goldie's foal went into a display of excited bucking.

The ride took them by lanes and woodland bridle ways until they came out at the road down across the golf course to the golden stretch of sand. It was still early enough for the beach to be quiet with just a few dog walkers out in the early sunlight and the breakers were quiet as well, just lapping gently up the shore in the slack of the tide. The horses' attentions focussed on the flat sand and the inviting space and Patsy said, 'We'll just go slowly until they've had time to settle.'

They trotted, going the length of the beach and as usual Patsy turned Golly to lead them to the water's edge. All the horses lowered their heads to sniff the gentle surf and Boy began to paw it over his legs. The family were laughing, letting their own mounts join in, and when they turned back to face the open beach even Colin looked excited.

'Are we going to gallop?' he asked, and Katy said 'Not on purpose but hang on.'

It started as a canter with Mack in the lead until the dog came flying after them and tearing alongside barking. Boy dived forward, swerved past Aries, and took off down the beach as Patsy yelled, 'steady, sit back.'

For a moment it looked as though she had lost them but Katy, who had been next in line, was pulling Lad up and the two cobs subsided as Golly, dropping back to a trot, came alongside. Colin was being run away with until Mack sent Aries after him and pulled across in front of Boy, forcing him into the water to slow him up and order has restored.

'Still boring?' Mack asked a scarlet faced Colin, who was breathlessly shortening his reins as Boy floundered out of the water. The dog's owners had grabbed him and the lady was apologising although the man with her was muttering objections about horses being on a public beach.

Colin, still breathless, shook his head as Boy also stopped to shake himself and the girls laughed. They were getting re-organised when there was a shout from higher up the beach and while Mack was talking to Colin Patsy saw a man hurrying towards them, a slender, dark haired young man dressed in jeans and a sleek black tee shirt. Mack had seen him as well and he said, 'I think I can guess who this is.'

 Behind him, watching from the edge of the dunes, was the boy who had recognised Aries last time they had been on this beach and suddenly Patsy also suspected who this would be. Aries's head had gone up and he was looking round.

'It is you have my horse,' the man was beside them, his hand reaching to the horse's nose, and Mack said, 'Van, I presume. I rather thought this was my horse now.'

Aries was clearly pleased to see him, reaching out to

nuzzle him, and the man said 'Giovanni, she called me Van. Are you then a riding school? That horse was not for sale. He is not suitable for this. You are the instructor, are you? He is not suitable for students.'

'We are not from a riding school,' Mack told him. 'And any horse abandoned at livery with no fees paid is legally available for sale to recover the cost.

The horses were restless, eager to keep going, and Patsy said, 'Can we finish this ride and then discuss this in the car park before someone gets into more trouble?'

'You go with him,' said Katy. 'I'll carry on to the cliffs and then bring this lot up.'

'So are you then in charge?' Van looked at her and suddenly smiled, his gaze appreciative.

'Lucky students', he said. 'If I had my horse I would also follow you.'

The dark Latin gaze was hot enough to make Katy blush and Patsy found that she understood quite a lot about "call me Iris."

Mack was turning Aries towards the exit ramp from the beach and Van's attention returned to the horse.

'The livery money was not owed,' he said. 'There was a mis understanding about it, and, about other things.'

Patsy headed for the ramp behind Mack and Van followed. The car park was busy now with families heading for the beach and the parents of their riders had set up a picnic area on a patch of sandy grass just beyond the bank which surrounded it.

They looked surprised to see them without the children and the father said, 'What have you done with the kids, drowned them?'

'They're having a final canter,' Patsy explained. 'While we talk to this gentleman about Mack's horse.'

'Which is actually my horse,' said Van firmly, and the children's mother looked at him and received a small bow and a smile which affected her much as it had Katy.

Mack had led Aries aside and was loosening his noseband to let him pick at the salty bits of grass and Van said, 'I see you care for him.'

'He's well worth it,' said Mack. 'And I bought him in good faith and I would be sorry to hear I was wrong. I think you need to explain, but not here. Come to our place later, when we've had time to ride back.'

Rather reluctantly Van agreed. He put his arms round Aries's neck and hugged him and the horse gave him a friendly shove with his nose. He watched with pricked ears as Van walked away and Katy, riding up from the beach with the visitors, exchanged another appreciative look with him. Mack, watching, said 'I think I can imagine what happened. That young man just can't help it. I've a feeling I might be going to lose my horse.'

Unhappily Patsy thought he might be right.

Van arrived at Bryn Uchaf soon after they got back. Rather aptly he was driving a small white van sign written with the name 'Luigi's' on it in black. The visitors had gone back to the cottage and Katy to fetch Tomos. The horses were turned out and Aries was grazing alongside Boy who had become his friend.

'I suppose I was the blame,' Van sounded embarrassed

as he began to explain. 'I was so pleased to find a safe place for my horse that my thinking was not clear. I think too it was the wrong thinking of the lady, perhaps she thought more was meant when I said sweet things to her...compliments...and more. She was alone, and she is an attractive lady...I did not pretend anything more.'

'But you slept with her,' said Mack bluntly. 'And let her think you were serious.'

Van had the grace to blush but he nodded and Mack sighed.

'Then she got possessive and you ran for it,' he said. 'What triggered that, was it something about smuggled alcohol?'

'I see Iris talked to you more,' he said. 'I was foolish to tell her, it was only the one time, my brother paid for a good bargain in brandy for the restaurant which he runs. She was anger with me when I would not commit to her, we had big anger and she was saying she would telephone the Garda. I went away but I thought she would still mind my horse.'

'So what made you risk coming back?' Mack asked him.

'My brother, he did not want his restaurant closed down so he admit and pay the duty and a fine,' Van told them. 'I did not think she would sell my horse, she should know I would return for him.'

'And what now?' asked Patsy. 'I take it you've thought about it. Did you plan to go back home with him?'

Van looked at her and suddenly treated her to his devastating smile.

'But I am come home,' he said. 'Iris is first angry but then very welcoming and I find now I do mean the things I say. But it will not be smoothed quite unless I have my horse back. She said you had bought in good faith, she would not tell where you were. Then my young beach friend phone and tell me you were there with him.'

Patsy knew Mack had no choice. He would not refuse to sell Aries back. He would be sorry but at least, thanks to Ana, he could still for the moment ride Osbourne.

'Maybe it's as well,' he said to Patsy later when Van had gone. 'Italy deserves an intrepid young rider, not an old has been like me. Those two suit each other, both willing to take risks. All I need is transport and the means of a bit of exercise.'

'I don't think "old has been" is being very fair on yourself,' Patsy told him. 'Not at all how I'd describe you. But I am afraid you'll have to give that Latin lover his horse back.'

Katy arrived home with her son on the patient Buzz and demanded to know what had happened. She agreed with the decision about Aries but said she wondered how long the reunion between Van and 'call me Iris' would last.

'She'll either need to keep him on a very short rein or just turn a blind eye,' she said. 'Life with something that hot will never be comfortable but I can certainly see the attraction.'

Van collected his horse next day driving Iris's small and efficient horse box. He gave Mack his money back with a generous interest for what he called 'the miss understanding' and Mack watched regretfully as his briefly owned purchase was driven away.

'Come on,' Patsy told him. 'Let's take our two old faithfuls up to the top. Thanks to Ana Osbourne can enjoy being your main transport up there again.'

Also thanks to Ana something had definitely changed in the new cottage. With the clearing and replacing of the hag stone the atmosphere, if not welcoming, was quiet and the work on it was going ahead smoothly. Ethan's wrist was mending although still strapped up and Forrest and his father were at the late stages of plastering and painting. Patsy and Rhianne spent a busy day in Swansea hunting down second-hand furnishing in good condition for the rooms and new kitchen and bathroom fittings were delivered. There was news too of the earlier visitors from the first cottage. A grateful letter from Myra enclosed a professional photo of Verity on Challenger winning a big class at Hickstead and saying that the change and variety of the riding with them had restored the horse's enthusiasm for the jumping and for life in general.

'There you are,' said Mack. 'Rhianne can add horse rehabilitation to her list of services.'

With the cottage almost ready Forrest set to work to clear enough land round it to make a garden.

Arriving there one morning with Tomos on the inevitable donkey Patsy found Rhianne looking at the now smooth area of bare earth. The only plants remaining were a bushy clump of lavender at the corner by the house and a still flourishing old bush of rosemary, both of which Brooke, who had been to look at her brother's work when she had been to ride Nell, told him that their mother would say should be left alone.

'She said there was enough ill feeling here without risking more,' Brooke told them. 'She's got this idea that herbs are sensitive.'

'I'll not be arguing with her,' Rhianne told Patsy. 'Those can stay, I'll fork around them, give them a bit of fresh soil to spread into.'

She went to get a garden fork while Patsy lifted Tomos off the donkey to play with his guardian collie. The little boy had a toss and fetch game started with the dog and Patsy was looking at the new lambs in their pen in the barn when Rhianne called her to look at something. She had a decaying piece of canvas feed bag out on the back step of the cottage and she was unwrapping something that had been inside it.

'Thought it was a rock I'd hit,' she said, 'but it was this.' She was spreading the sacking out and something glinted in the sun. A horseshoe, one of four, burnished to a shine which had lasted inside the wrapping. Patsy stared.

'Whatever...?' she asked, and Rhianne picked one up.

'Big ones,' she said. 'They'd not be cob shoes. John's gramp used to have big horses, for the farm work.'

'But why would anyone bury them?' asked Patsy.

'John might know,' Rhianne put the shoe back with the others. 'I've a feeling this might give us some answers. He'll be in for his snack just now, come in and we'll show him.'

She picked Tomos up and led the way into the house.

John was seated at the kitchen table with a mug of tea when they went in and Rhianne laid the shoes out in front of him.

'Buried they were,' she told him. 'Under an old bush. And burnished and greased to save them. Now why would anyone be doing that?'

John picked one of the big shoes up and ran a finger round the curve, looking thoughtful.

'Blodyn,' he said. 'Blossom. Grampi used to talk sometimes about a big old plough horse he had, champion she was in the ploughing matches. Well known, he was, for his big horses. Used to take them to break and get them working. I mind him telling me of that one, showed me a photo once of her but I only saw it the once. Something happened to her I think.'

'I think I might be able to put a hand on that photo,' Rhianne handed round some of her home-made Welsh cakes and headed for the stairs. 'Wait now while I look.'

Like most of the old farmhouses this one had a loft and they heard the ladder clatter down. Patsy broke Tomos's Welsh cake into bits as the least messy way of giving it to him and Rhianne was back a few minutes later with an old envelope.

'This is the old man with one of his horses,' she said. 'And that will be the boy he had working with him. He and his Mam would likely have lived in that cottage. Some gossip there had been at the time about it, her not being married. The old man had quite a reputation, my Mam was a bit against me marrying John here in case he turned out to be something of the same mind.'

She smiled at him and bent to brush his cheek with her lips and for a moment Patsy caught a glimpse of an old, lasting passion.

The photograph was an old sepia one of a handsome dark-haired man with bright eyes and a crooked smile, dressed in work clothes of an older time. Beside him was a smiling boy with curly hair and between the two of them was a huge cart horse with a braided mane and luxuriously feathered legs.

'That's grandfather Rees and that will be the boy,' Rhianne told Patsy. 'Quite a reputation Rees had with his horse breaking and other things, hearts maybe. And the boy has his look.'

It suddenly made things a lot clearer, thought Patsy, perhaps a woman with an illegitimate son becoming an embarrassment, a son who loved the horses and hated to leave them. It could certainly be a cause for resentment.

'But why the shoes?' she asked. 'From a favourite perhaps, some sort of a memory? Or maybe one that died.'

'Ragwort,' said John suddenly. 'I remember now, ragwort it was that poisoned that good mare, ragwort missed in the hay making. Careless, a boy working here was. Grandfather told me that story as a way of giving me a warning about how dangerous that stuff is, always wanting me checking the fields, though it doesn't bother sheep as much.'

'And if that boy got the blame, maybe an excuse to get rid of an embarrassment, turn the boy and his maybe demanding Mam out of the cottage...now that's a cause for resentment sure enough,' said Rhianne. 'But it's all things we'll never know the whole of now'.

'What will you do with them?' Patsy asked, and Rhianne touched one of the shiny surfaces with her fingers.

'Put them back where they were,' she said. 'As Ana told you rosemary is for remembrance and I think that was why someone was putting them there.'

She and Patsy went back to the new garden and Rhianne made a deeper hole close under the bush and placed the shoes, wrapped now in a plastic bag, into it and shovelled the soil back over them.

'Surely with the witch stone over the door and the memory safe it should be calm here now,' she said, and Patsy hoped that she would be right.

CHAPTER ELEVEN

Osbourne was still comfortable on Ana's paste but Mack was conscious that too much work could do more damage to his stiffening joints and he regretted having had to give Aries back. Then he received a phone call from "Call me Iris".

'She says if I'm still looking for a horse she's got something needing a home' he told Patsy. 'She said it's hardly another Aries but it's the right sort of size and only a six-year-old. I said I'd have a look.'

'And see how the Van situation is going,' Patsy was curious to find out about that.

On her way to Tesco she had driven past the attractive looking little Italian restaurant called Luigi's and been glad to see that it looked to be flourishing.

Iris looked well. There was something subtly different about her, her blond hair looked a little less smartly controlled and she wore a tight-fitting blue shirt with the top buttons unfastened. She also looked relaxed and quite a lot younger. There was a pair of man's trainers on the step and as they turned to follow her down the yard Mack said softly 'All looks to be well.'

There was a grey head over a stable door, pricked ears watching them approach, and Iris said, 'That's the horse, not much like that racehorse of Van's but he could fill the gap.'.

She opened the door and the horse backed up, looking anxious. He was a tall, rather ungainly looking animal at first glance with a head showing quality but plenty of bone There was a touch of feather above large hooves and a thick, darker tail but with a thin neck and bony hips. He was grey but with brown spots like freckles running all through his rather rough coat. Iris patted him and he relaxed enough to put an inquiring head down to search her hands.

'Some blood but I think there's some pony in there as well,' she said. 'Maybe Highland from that colour and that thick dark tail. As you might guess he was a rescue case, abandoned in a rough bit of field after the girl who owned him decided she was keener on some man than on being a show jumper. She took off leaving her parents to cope, which they didn't. The mother saw me riding and heard I did a bit of dealing and asked me to take him over. I gather the girl is now pregnant and living in Cardiff.'

"Another unfortunate attraction responsible there as well," thought Patsy. "But perhaps Iris's was not unfortunate after all. She certainly looked well on it."

'I suppose he's rideable,' Mack was looking doubtful. The horse was a big change from Aries but seeing the large, honest eyes and look of strength in the powerful limbs Patsy felt that there was a lot to like.

'Yes, apparently he rides better than he looks,' Iris told them. 'Van tried him. It was him who suggested you. Said he's a bit unconventional like that horse of his.

He'd heard a story about you saving some girl on a horse from getting into trouble in the estuary and he thought you deserved a replacement for his animal.'

Mack had joined her in the horse's box and was smoothing his neck while the horse's ears flickered what looked hopefully towards him.

'Do I need to ask his name,' he said and Iris laughed.

'You're probably guessing right,' she said. 'Freckles.'

'Can I try him?' asked Mack and Iris said she would get some tack.

The horse stiffened a bit when the saddle went on and rather unwillingly opened his mouth for the snaffle bit.

'I think he's had someone too casual about tacking him up,' said Iris. 'Banging his teeth, wrenching up the girth, that sort of thing. Good saddle, though, jumping style, shame the girl's interests got diverted.'

They stood aside and Iris led the horse out.

'He's pretty straight I think,' she told Mack, as he prepared to mount. 'A bit too anxious to please if anything.'

She opened the gate into the same field in which he had tried Van's horse and this horse went through with a rush, turning his ears back to get a feel of this new rider.

Mack rode in his usual un-demanding style with a long rein and quiet legs and when the horse broke into a rather jerky trot he let him go forward. Patsy soon saw what Iris meant about him being anxious to please, any movement of Mack's hands on the reins or touch with his legs had him starting forward or hastily stopping and his ears were constantly on the move as he waited for the next signal but gradually he began to relax. He moved unexpectedly well, straight and free striding, and when he cantered he lost most of his anxious look and went readily forward.

'Do you know anything about what he's done,' asked Patsy.

'The mother said the girl used to go out on him, the road past the field was quite busy so he's probably all right in traffic,' Iris told her. 'And she said he won something jumping in a local show. He could be quite a useful animal when he gets some sort of real condition on him. Oh, and he had a vet's certificate when the girl bought him at Llanybydder sales.'

'That's where my cob mare came from,' Patsy remembered Goldie, half wild and in foal, in the midst of the crowded sale yard. You could buy anything equine there from a rough coated youngster which could develop into a champion right down to sad, unwanted old workers and mountain foals bound for the butcher.

Mack rode back to the gate with the horse looking happier and nodded.

'He's got a nice feel,' he said. 'I wouldn't mind seeing how he made out. What do you want for him?'

'I told his owner in this state and with no provenance it would be a matter of hundreds, if that,' said Iris. 'But all she really wanted was to have him off her hands.'

'Five, then,' said Mack. 'And this time no strings. Alright with you Patsy? He can always go back to the sales.'

"Like Not," thought Patsy, who knew perfectly well that however hard hearted he sounded once the horse was with them he was likely to be staying. Iris was nodding.

'Fair enough,' she said. 'Never know, you might be buying a show jumper.'

Mack laughed and patted the horse. 'Not my line,' he said. 'So long as he doesn't dump me too often on the hill he'll do. He feels as though he deserves a better chance than whatever he's been used to.'

He rode Freckles back to his stable and Iris offered them coffee while he transferred the money by phone into her account. Patsy asked carefully if Van was more settled now and Iris's laugh sounded slightly embarrassed.

'It seems so,' she said. 'We really did get our wires a bit tangled. Good of you to be so understanding about the horse.'

They heard a car drive in and a few minutes later Van came into the room, dark and dashing and bringing with him an air of vibrating warmth. He went straight to give Iris a kiss which left no doubt about the promise behind it and asked Mack how he had liked the horse.

'A change from yours but I hope he'll do the job,' Mack told him, and Van looked pleased. He and Iris wasted no time in last goodbyes and Iris said she would bring Freckles over the next day.

'I wonder how long before that situation cools down,' said Mack, as they turned into the narrow cliff road for home, but Patsy had a feeling that a point had been reached and settled and it could be quite a long time.

Freckles was a success. He loved the moor, striding out easily over the rough ground and tackling the hills with sure footed ease. He was not fazed by steams and ditches and took small gorse bushes in his stride in a way that showed he knew something about jumping.

'I think Iris was right about him having some Highland pony in him,' said Patsy, after Freckles had happily led the way down the steep sunken track from the high rocks and Mack agreed. Even Golly had slipped a couple of times. Mack's new mount rapidly accepted his relaxed way of riding, liking the long rein and answering easily when he did tighten them.

'He may not be another Aries but he's going to keep me my roaming time,' said Mack, as they headed for home.

Freckles fitted in easily with the other horses, accepting their pecking order and quietly making friends with Osbourne, seeming to recognise a sympathetic character, and after some startled snorting and staring he accepted the donkeys. It seemed that Mack's horse problems were settled for the moment.

The cottage problems seemed to have eased as well. Progress was going ahead with it, the fittings were in and the final touches of painting done. Cheerful flowery curtains went up when the rooms were furnished. Ana came to sense the feel of it and to make a few adjustments to the placing of some furniture and the addition of two green, ferny plants on windowsills.

'There's still something lacking,' she said. 'There's an emptiness that needs filling before anything else can creep in. It needs life, happiness, perhaps love under its roof.'

It sounded fairly simple but unless Rhianne could let it as a honeymoon cottage Patsy did not see how it could be achieved.

'Get Iris and her Latin lover to stay in it.' Mack was half serious but Patsy was not sure if that relationship would be quite the right thing.

'Stay there yourselves,' suggested Katy. 'You still behave like young lovers at times anyway.' but

Patsy thought that was hardly the right answer either. Ethan had received a text and photo from Summer showing her riding in an outdoor arena, one of a group in a lesson. They were trotting and Summer looked happy.

'An hour or so off from being nagged,' she texted. 'Not so much fun as riding with Patsy though. I just wish I could plan a gap year doing this, but not much hope. It looks like I'm to be shovelled off to Uni straight from school as my grades were good enough.'

'I suppose she could refuse to go,' Patsy said to Mack. 'But Tabs could give her a hard time if she did. Flynn should back her up but the same goes for him.'

'Yes, it takes some nerve to stand up to Tabs,' agreed. Mack wryly. 'As I well know.'

Arriving at Rhianne's with Tomos on the donkey a couple of mornings later Patsy found that Muff, playing one of her usual tricks, had slipped out and followed them. By the time Rhianne had come out to meet them the little mule had disappeared.

'Gone exploring, likely,' said Rhianne, and Patsy put Buzz in his enclosure and went to look.

There was no sign of Muff in the old orchard or the yard but going round the corner towards the new cottage Patsy saw the little white shape hesitating on the newly laid doorstep. The door was open and as she started hurriedly towards it Patsy saw the little mule's big ears go forward and she stepped inside.

'Muff,' Patsy hurried after her, expecting a sudden crash as the mule entered the kitchen, but there was nothing. By the time she got inside Muff was nowhere in sight but there was a hoarse half bray from the new living room, the part of the old building that had once been the stable, and Patsy hurried after it.

Muff was there, eating one of Ana's plants, her ears still forward and her head tilted as if someone was stroking her. Watching Patsy knew that she should not interfere. She heard Rhianne following her and waved her back and it was Tomos who broke through, running past his grandmothers and laughing as he saw the mule.

'Boy find her,' he said, as Muff turned towards him, and for a second Patsy saw something there, just a soft shadow at the mule's head, and then it was gone. Tomos was hugging Muff and beside Patsy his guardian sheep dog followed him with the hair standing up along her back. The cottage was suddenly lit by a shaft of sunlight slanting through the window and Tomos looked round, puzzled.

'Gone,' he said. 'He was nice, Muff thought so.'

'Yes,' agreed Patsy, taking his hand. 'I think she did. I tell you what Tomos, if we get a mat to cover the carpet we could let her stay for a bit and perhaps we could have our lunch in here, if Nanna two doesn't mind.'

Muff pricked up her ears again and brayed with an almost full voice instead of her usual croak, and Patsy was sure that someone was laughing. Could that be what was needed, could the last shade of resentment be taken away by Muff, who had been hurt here, coming back of her own accord?

Rhianne laughed but agreed to a picnic.

'Christening it, you could say,' she said, and when she brought pasties and rolls and a hardboiled egg for Tomos and sliced carrots and apples for Muff she also brought a bottle of wine. Patsy phoned Mack and Katy to join them, Ethan came in looking for Muff, whom he had seen arrive, and John and Gareth came in from the sheep. Muff joined in happily, eating her own picnic and then going round receiving tit bits from everyone before wandering back outside to find Buzz patiently waiting. Rhianne had even brought glasses and now she shared out the wine between them.

'Shame it is there's not more,' she said. 'But fair play, I wasn't to know we'd be holding a party.'

'A toast,' said Mack, raising his glass. 'To Blossom Cottage and to all who sail in her.'

'Yes,' said Rhianne. 'That has to be the name. I'll get a good sign made for it.'

'And here's a libation,' Mack tipped the last drops from his glass onto the hearth. 'To light any dark places and quiet the shades.'

And it seemed to Patsy that the room was suddenly lighter, although it could have been because a shaft of sunlight came after a passing cloud.

Later that day the weather changed, rain blowing in with thickening cloud, and by evening it was blowing hard, a typical western hill country summer storm. In the fields the horses were sheltering against the hedges and Patsy considered bringing some of them in but it was not cold and in the end she just brought Muff in as she might still be fragile from pneumonia, and Buzz as company for her.

It was a noisy night with rain driving against the windows and the doors and loft trap door rattling from the gusts and once Patsy heard Buzz braying in the stable. Beside her Mack stirred and Patsy sleepily wondered if she should investigate.

'And come back half drowned,' Mack pulled her closer to him and Patsy felt her slight anxiety fade at his touch. It was still new enough in her life to feel like this, the deep, melting warmth and rising need and she let herself relax into it as his hand slid down to her thigh. The donkey would soon let them know if there was anything to worry about.

The storm had blown away by morning, losing its force over the more inland hills, and when Patsy did go outside there was a mist rising from the fields as the sun drew the wet up from the land. The horses were basking in it, steam rising from their coats, and in the stable Buzz brayed again. Going inside Patsy saw him watching for her, Muff close to his side, and in the

hay store at the end something else was stirring.
'What...?' Patsy started towards it, staring, as a figure sat up, a horse rug slipping off the shoulders of a girl with tangled dark hair and a dirt-streaked face.
'Summer,' exclaimed Patsy.
Summer it was, Flynn's daughter and Tabitha's stepdaughter, wearing a hay encrusted blue sweater, a soaked jacket thrown over the partition beside her.
'Hello Patsy,' there was the remembered defensive hint in her voice and she stumbled stiffly as she stood up. 'I...I'd love a cup of coffee if you'd let me in.'
'There was a terrible row,' she told Patsy and Mack after a hot shower and the loan of one of Katy's sweaters and some jeans. 'Dad told Tabs he thought the uni business should be up to me, if I wanted to put it off and try to find an alternative I should and she went wild, saying she wanted their life back, she didn't intend to have her home like a hotel for someone expecting room service all the time. Then he started on it being his home as well and when she started throwing things I'd had enough. I've got my car now so I just got in and set off. I didn't know what to do but I thought of Ethan, and you, and the horses, so I just headed this way.'
'How did you get so wet?' Patsy asked her. 'Have you left the car somewhere?'
'It's electric,' said Summer. 'It ran out of charge, just off the motorway. I'd never driven on a motorway before, it was really scary, and then it started bleeping about needing charging, and I'd had enough. I was passing a service place and there was a lorry pulling in with a

Fishguard address on it. I dumped the car and found the driver filling up and begged a lift.'

'Summer,' Patsy remembered horror stories of what happened to girls hitch hiking. 'You should have called me. One of us would have collected you and got your car on charge.'

'It was alright,' Summer told her. 'He was really nice, he even knew who you were. He said his kids loved the dancing mule. He was coming right past the turn for here, he would have brought me all the way, but it was a very long lorry, he thought it might get stuck. I walked the last bit but it was so late. I was going to knock but then I heard Buzz and it was nice and warm in there so I decided to wait for morning.'

'And now you'll call your Dad,' Patsy told her. 'I'm surprised he hasn't rung himself, he must guess you'd come here.'

'He thinks I'm at my friend's house,' Summer looked defensive. 'That's where I told them I was going.'

'By now they probably know it wasn't true,' Mack sounded firm. 'You ring Flynn now, before he starts a search.'

Summer looked as if she was about to argue but Mack's expression told her it would not be a good idea and she got up to find her phone in the pocket of her wet coat.

Flynn was relieved and Summer said he was not as angry as she had expected.

'He's going to come here,' she said. 'He said he'd check my car on the way, he's got the spare keys. I can collect it on the way home. He promised to talk seriously about what I can do about everything.'

'What sort of job do you want, if you can choose?' Patsy asked her. 'In door or out?'
'Outside,' said Summer at once, 'with animals... horses, but not just mucking out and I don't think I'd want to teach kids to ride.'

'What about breeding?' Katy had joined them now and discovered what was going on. 'Maybe try helping out at a stud farm.'
She raised her eyebrows at her mother and Patsy remembered Angie Shaw and her pregnant groom.
'Breeding? Foals and beautiful stallions like Fly?' Summer looked interested. 'Oh yes, something like that would be great.'
'And we might know just the place where you could try it out,' Patsy told her.

CHAPTER TWELVE

Evan Flynn thought it a good idea. He arrived with his usual clatter and revving across the cattle grid and he was obviously relieved to find his daughter in one piece although he was also angry with her. He looked sleeker than he had while he was living in Mack's old house and recovering from a close brush with death from Covid. His slightly greying fair hair was expertly cut and would add dash to his personality. At present he was working as a dancer and choreographer with a big west end musical but there was a slightly strained look in his face which Patsy suspected was the result of a hectic life with his two females. He agreed to Patsy phoning Angie to see if she seriously wanted someone. It seemed that she did.

'Even before their head girl went on leave she says she was thinking of finding a working pupil,' Patsy told them. 'It would be a living in job, of course, there's a staff cottage where her head girl lives. It could lead on to a specialist course in stud work. I told her you'd go and talk to her.'

'I can't thank you enough,' Flynn told Patsy, when they were ready to leave. 'It should make my life a whole lot smoother, give Tabs and me a chance to get ourselves back on an even keel, and I'll know there's someone round here to keep an eye on things.'

"As we will," thought Patsy. "Even if it is being taken for granted."

And there was another thing, which Summer reminded her of when her father had gone ahead to the car,

'Ethan will be pleased,' she said. 'We can see each other properly now.'

She went happily after Flynn leaving Patsy feeling that another possible problem had just been dumped on her shoulders. However as she watched Flynn, turning to say goodbye to Katy run his fingers appreciatively through her hair, she knew that at least distance would prevent a different problem from developing there.

The new sign went up and the first visitors for the cottage arrived, a family with two girls who wanted to ride. They were both fairly experienced. Rather anxiously, after the first lively canter up past Hafod, Patsy dared to ask them how they liked the cottage.

'It's fab,' one of them told her. 'Really snug and we like the name. Rhianne said it was called after a horse. Do you know, we both dreamed about horses last night, big ones, it must be because she told us that Blossom was a ploughing horse.'

'Funny though,' said her sister. 'We both woke up, really early, and we thought we heard a horse whickering, like they do when they see someone coming with feeds. And there was a lovely smell like hay.'

Smiling to herself Patsy decided not to comment. If there was an echo from anything it sounded a comfortable one.

It was full summer now. In the fields the grass was tall and thick, silvery with the heads of seed, and hay making had begun. A week later, high on the moor for once with no visitors, Patsy and Mack stopped their horses to savour the sweet warmth and the green and golden view. Skylarks were singing, soaring from their nests in the heather, a red kite glided above on the warm rising air, and Rhianne's cottages were happily busy with a new input of holiday families. For the moment they could all relax.

'There were times,' said Mack. 'When I thought my days of riding up here might be numbered, but this fellow has given me hope I was wrong.'

He patted the speckled horse's neck and Freckles turned his head briefly from staring out across the moor to nuzzle his foot.

'And thanks to Ana you've still got the old boy going,' Patsy reminded him.

'Yes,' Mack grinned. 'We owe quite a bit to our local witch and her family. Even magical Muff is thanks to Forrest and his horse stealing efforts which brought us her Mum.'

They turned their horses back towards home and Patsy, following his horse's now rounding quarters on her much-loved Golly, knew that he was right. Muff had proved a catalyst in many ways.

The end.

Printed in Great Britain
by Amazon